THE SPIRITUAL WISDOM

OF IF:

A DEVOTIONAL GUIDE BASED UPON

KIPLING'S CLASSIC POEM, RELATED SCRIPTURES,

AND BIBLICAL PERSONALITIES

By Dr. J. Rodney Short

Portions of this book were published in
The Wisdom of If:
Master the Essence of Kipling's Inspirational Poem
and Change Your Life

J. Rodney Short
Copyright © 2011

&

An Interactive Companion to The Wisdom of If:
Let Kipling's Inspirational Poem Guide You Toward Serenity,
Courage, and Wisdom

J. Rodney Short
Copyright © 2011

Other Publications

Barnibee, The Amazing Bumblebee

J. Rodney Short
Copyright © 2011

"Because anyone who wants to approach God must believe both that He exists and that He cares enough to respond to those who seek Him."
Hebrews 6:11 (MSG)

§ § §

Remember:

When trying to grasp the awesomeness of God, you cannot always think logically.

Copyright © 2012 by Dr. J. Rodney Short

Design and Layout: Sally Vaughn
Cover Design: Crystal Wood

ISBN 978-0-9850733-2-9

Printed in the United States of America

© All rights reserved. No part of this publication may be reproduced or transmitted in any form or by any means, electronic or mechanical, including photocopy, recording, or any information storage and retrieval system, without permission in writing from the author.

All Scripture quotations in this book are from the following translations:

New American Standard Bible (NASB) © 1960, 1962, 1963, 1971, 1973, 1975, and 1977 by the Lockman Foundation.
Used by permission.

The Living Bible (TLB), copyright © 1971 by Tyndale House Publishers, Wheaton, Ill. Used by permission.

The New International Version of the Bible (NIV), copyright © 1983 by the International Bible Society. Used by permission of Zondervan Bible Publishers.

The Message (MSG), copyright © by Eugene H. Peterson, 1993, 1994, 1995, 1996. Used by permission of NavPress Publishing Group.

The King James Version of the Bible (KJV).

Holy Bible, New Living Translation (NLT) (Wheaton, Ill.: Tyndale House Publishers, 1996). Used by permission.

New King James Version (NKJV), copyright © 1979, 1980, 1982, by Thomas Nelson, Inc. Used by permission.

Published by:
JRSK Books
Dallas/Denton
www.jrskbooks.com
1120 Ellison Park Circle
Denton, TX 76205

Dedication

To all of those who are striving to live
by the Christlike virtues and behaviors
described in the life-altering
and inspirational poem "If,"
and
to my mother who loved me
unconditionally.

ACKNOWLEDGEMENTS

To Sharon Key and her creative Sunday School class for sharing with me how they used an early draft of this book to invigorate their Bible study and enhance their lives.

To Keith Shelton, DeeAnna Oliveira, Aaron Claycomb, and Erin Marissa Russell for their suggestions and editorial comments.

To Dr. Larry Reynolds, a retired pastor, for his critique and spiritual insights.

To my former students, who have shared with me how much this poem has meant to them.

To pastor Ralph Mann for his insights on the Investment Parable.

And, last but not least,
to Sally Vaughn, who has been a major influence in all my book efforts. Sally, thank you for your calmness, wise counsel, exemplary computer skills, and for being the person God called you to be.

If

If you can keep your head when all about you
  Are losing theirs and blaming it on you;
If you can trust yourself when all men doubt you,
  But make allowance for their doubting too:
If you can wait and not be tired by waiting,
  Or, being lied about, don't deal in lies,
Or, being hated, don't give way to hating,
  And yet don't look too good, nor talk too wise;

If you can dream – and not make dreams your master;
  If you can think – and not make thoughts your aim,
If you can meet with Triumph and Disaster
  And treat those two impostors just the same:
If you can bear to hear the truth you've spoken
  Twisted by knaves to make a trap for fools,
Or watch the things you gave your life to, broken,
  And stoop and build'em up with worn-out tools;

If you can make one heap of all your winnings
  And risk it on one turn of pitch-and-toss,
And lose, and start again at your beginnings,
  And never breathe a word about your loss:
If you can force your heart and nerve and sinew
  To serve your turn long after they are gone,
And so hold on when there is nothing in you
  Except the Will which says to them: "Hold on!"

If you can talk with crowds and keep your virtue,
  Or walk with Kings – nor lose the common touch,
If neither foes nor loving friends can hurt you,
  If all men count with you, but none too much:
If you can fill the unforgiving minute
  With sixty seconds' worth of distance run,
Yours is the Earth and everything that's in it,
  And – which is more – you'll be a Man, my son!

- Rudyard Kipling (1910)

Table of Contents

Introduction	1
The Spiritual Hall of Fame	9
Stanza One	16
Chapter 1	
"If you can keep your head when all about you are losing theirs and blaming it on you;"	17
Moses Could	
Chapter 2	
"If you can trust yourself when all men doubt you, but make allowance for their doubting too:"	24
Daniel Could	
Chapter 3	
"If you can wait and not be tired by waiting,"	29
Jacob Could	
Chapter 4	
"Or, being lied about, don't deal in lies,"	34
Stephen Could	
Chapter 5	
"Or, being hated, don't give way to hating,"	39
Joseph Could	
Chapter 6	
"And yet don't look too good, or talk too wise;"	45
David and Abigail Could	
Stanza Two	51
Chapter 7	
"If you can dream –and not make dreams your master; if you can think–and not make thoughts your aim."	52
Nehemiah Could	

CHAPTER 8
"IF YOU CAN MEET WITH TRIUMPH AND DISASTER
AND TREAT THOSE TWO IMPOSTORS JUST THE SAME:" 57
PAUL COULD

CHAPTER 9
"IF YOU CAN BEAR TO HEAR THE TRUTH YOU'VE SPOKEN
TWISTED BY KNAVES TO MAKE A TRAP FOR FOOLS," 62
JESUS COULD

CHAPTER 10
"OR WATCH THE THINGS YOU GAVE YOUR LIFE TO, BROKEN,
AND STOOP AND BUILD 'EM UP WITH WORN-OUT TOOLS;" 67
JOB COULD

STANZA THREE 74
CHAPTER 11
"IF YOU CAN MAKE ONE HEAP OF ALL YOUR WINNINGS
AND RISK IT ON ONE TURN OF PITCH-AND-TOSS,
AND LOSE, AND START AGAIN AT YOUR BEGINNINGS,
AND NEVER BREATHE A WORD ABOUT YOUR LOSS;" 75
THE DISCIPLES COULD/INVESTMENT PARABLE

CHAPTER 12
"IF YOU CAN FORCE YOUR HEART AND NERVE AND SINEW
TO SERVE YOUR TURN LONG AFTER THEY ARE GONE,
AND SO HOLD ON WHEN THERE IS NOTHING IN YOU
EXCEPT THE WILL WHICH SAYS TO THEM: 'HOLD ON!'" 81
PAUL COULD

STANZA FOUR 86
CHAPTER 13
"IF YOU CAN TALK WITH CROWDS AND KEEP YOUR VIRTUE,
OR WALK WITH KINGS—NOR LOSE THE COMMON TOUCH," 87
ESTHER COULD

CHAPTER 14
"IF NEITHER FOES NOR LOVING FRIENDS CAN HURT YOU
IF ALL MEN COUNT WITH YOU, BUT NONE TOO MUCH:" 94
JESUS AND PAUL UNDERSTOOD THIS

CHAPTER 15
"IF YOU CAN FILL THE UNFORGIVING MINUTE
WITH SIXTY SECONDS' WORTH OF DISTANCE RUN,"   100
RUTH AND NAOMI COULD

CHAPTER 16
YOURS IS THE EARTH AND EVERYTHING THAT'S IN IT,
"AND—WHICH IS MORE—YOU'LL BE A MAN, MY SON!"   106

IN CLOSING   112
NOTES   113
ABOUT THE AUTHOR   114
IF   115

IF

YOU FOLLOW GOD'S WISDOM, YOU CAN BECOME THE PERSON YOU WERE MEANT TO BE.

"Coincidence is God's way of remaining anonymous."

Albert Einstein

Introduction

The poem "If" by Rudyard Kipling has been translated into 27 languages, read by millions, and has influenced countless people of all ages. It is arguably the most famous inspirational poem in the English language and is considered a classic. Why? Because "If" is a wisdom-filled composite of life-altering rules of conduct and virtues that, if acquired and acted upon, can change your life forever for the better. In essence, it is a poem about the road to maturity and self-control, about mountains to climb and goals to meet, and about facing conflicts in life and overcoming them. *And for some people, it is a poem that moves them closer to God.*

<u>Some Background</u>

For over 20 years I incorporated this poem into my lectures to graduate classes and in speeches that I gave across the country. Many of my graduate students and seminar participants have shared with me that they believe this poem has a ***spiritual*** dimension. A majority of my students have collectively said to me, "I do not know if Kipling was spiritual or not, but his poem 'If' is." Many people would agree with this assessment. And one of them was Winston Churchill. He even called "If" his spiritual autobiography.* Many have also suggested to me that this life-altering poem met a need in their life and inspired them when they needed inspiring.

---

*See my book *A Unique Look at Kipling's Poem "If"* for a more in-depth discussion and citations on how this poem influenced me, Churchill, and many other eminent people.

THE SPIRITUAL WISDOM OF IF

"If" for example inspired, Dr. Charles Swindoll, a nationally recognized pastor, author, scholar, radio evangelist, and former Marine. He wrote in his inspiring book on Esther that the words in "If" are "immortal." "If" also inspired Dr. Morris Sheats, a dynamic pastor and founder of several churches in the Dallas area. He said that, next to Scripture, the poem "If" has been his mainstay since he was a student at Monterey High School in Lubbock, Texas. (Mine too.)

§§§

As I study the Bible, I am convinced that this wisdom-filled poem is aligned with the Biblical Word (Scriptures). As I have noted, thousands have attested to the wisdom and common sense embedded in this poem. King Solomon wrote in Proverbs 3:21, "Have two goals: wisdom – that is, knowing and doing right – and common sense. Don't let them slip away, for they fill you with living energy and are a feather in your cap. They keep you from defeat and disaster and from stumbling off the trail." (TLB)

> "I strive to live a spiritual life and this poem nourishes my spirituality. It stands out for me as one of the greatest poems ever written."
>
> Jackie Reed,
> Former Student

With this Scripture in mind, I can promise you (as did Kipling) that if you acquire and act upon the behaviors and virtues described in "If" and the related Scriptures that I have included in this book, your chances of avoiding disaster greatly diminished and your chances of living with energy and success are greatly enhanced.

But, before we proceed, let's look briefly at the remarkable man who wrote this timeless, classic poem …

A Sketch of Kipling's Life
§§§

- Rudyard Kipling came into this world through a very difficult childbirth.
- His mother was in labor with him for six days – a probable cause for the very poor eyesight that was to afflict him later in life.
- At the age of five and a half, Rudyard and his sister, Trix, age three, were sent to England to board with Harry and Rosa Holloway. They were not to see their parents for five years.
- Mrs. Holloway afflicted both mental and physical abuse on Rudyard.
- He was constantly told he was dumb, stupid, and would never amount to anything.
- He was beaten by her.
- Once he was sent to school with a placard that read, "Kipling is a liar."
- At 13, he was sent to a military school where the students nicknamed him "Beetle" because of the shape of his head.
- At 15, he was sent to the dungeon for two days for tearing up school reports.
- Because of his fear of Mrs. Holloway, Kipling developed a severe case of insomnia that haunted him all of his life.
- While on a trip to the United States in 1899, his six-year-old daughter, Josephine, developed pneumonia and died.
- His only son, John, was killed in World War I, and his body was never found.

But …

Was Kipling an overcomer? Was he an achiever?
The Answer is YES!

- … In his early twenties, he achieved worldwide recognition for a collection of verses and short stories he published.
- … In 1907, he was awarded the Nobel Prize for Literature.
- … He received an honorary degree from the University of Oxford along with Mark Twain.
- … In 1923, he was made Rector of St. Andrew's University in Scotland.
- … He became a successful writer of poetry, short stories, children's tales, novels, articles, and an autobiography.
- … Several of his children's books were made into movies.
- … At age 60, he was featured on the cover of *Time* magazine in the September 27, 1926, issue.

AN INTRODUCTION TO KIPLING

Challenges That Can Make a Difference

Before I proceed, let me issue these challenges to you if you want to live the inspired and meaningful life. First seek God! Then seek His wisdom and His purpose for your life. Then learn to be content and at peace with yourself. Know the Word. Meditate on the Scriptures I have included in this book that I believe correlate with the maxims (rules to live by) and virtues in "If." <u>Memorize them</u> so that you can call upon them in your time of need. "Only then will you prosper and succeed in all you do" (Joshua 1:8 NLT). Remember, nothing is more important than seeking God's wisdom when you are trying to make the right choice about some event or circumstance in your life.

> The Bible helps us keep things in perspective. Especially study and reflect upon the nuggets of wisdom that are found in the books of Proverbs and Ecclesiastes.

One of my Goals

With the importance of seeking God's wisdom and meditating and acting upon the Word (Scriptures) acknowledged, one of my goals in writing this book is to help you internalize and act upon the embedded spiritual wisdom found in this classic 32-line poem. And one of the best ways for you to start acquiring this wisdom is for you to memorize it. I did; you can.

> As I pen these words, my ten-year-old granddaughter Macy Grace Fox is memorizing this character-building poem.

To help you do this,

THE SPIRITUAL WISDOM OF IF

I have included a copy of the poem on the last page of the book that you can cut out and post or carry with you. Then after you have memorized "If," I want you to recall appropriate lines and related Scriptures when you are faced with a tough choice or decision that could impact your life. This mental effort will help you make better choices or decisions.

Keep in mind that Kipling wrote this poem to his 12-year-old son John in 1910, hoping that it would provide him with a framework that would help shape his values and guide him toward maturity and adulthood.* He tried to base these values on the conduct, attitudes, and behavior of wise men he had known, admired, and respected.

> "Train a child in the way he should go,
> and when he is old he will not turn from it."
> Proverbs 22:6 (NIV)

The author of Proverbs reminds us, as did Kipling, how important it is to surround ourselves with wise people when he wrote, "He who walks with the wise grows wise, but a companion of fools suffers harm" (Proverbs 13:20 NIV). Thousands of years later C.S. Lewis echoed Solomon's insight with this powerful insightful, "The next best thing to being wise oneself is to live in a circle of those who are." (Oh, so true!)

> "God constantly uses the lives of Bible characters to teach us, to encourage us, to warn us."
> Dr. Charles R. Swindoll,
> *A Man of Integrity and Forgiveness: Joseph*

With Solomon's and Lewis' wise advice in mind, I am trying to look at the conduct and attitudes of a few heroic and wise, **but imperfect**, men and women in the

---

*If this wisdom-filled poem sounds sexist, remember that it was published in 1910. Do not let this keep you from looking for the universal truths found in the poem.

Bible to see what we can learn from them in relation to the virtues Kipling outlined in "If." There was no rhyme or reason for the examples I used. They simply inspired and energized me. In some cases, the Biblical personalities I used could easily be examples of more than one line or couplet in the poem. For example, I have used the apostle Paul several times as an example of a particular virtue.

We also need to keep in mind that the Bible is an emotionally stirring book because it is filled with the drama of people's lives. For God pulls no punches with the men and women in the Bible. He notes their warts, as well as their strengths.

The Bible also reminds us that many of them lived unsavory and sinful lives. They were real people, just like you and me. They had their moral flaws. For example, Abraham was a liar, Isaac and Jacob were both poor fathers, Jacob was also a schemer and a cheat, Rahab was a prostitute, David was an adulterer and murderer, Peter had a temper, Paul was an accomplice to a murder, Noah got drunk, and Jonah ran from God. But, God used these ordinary people to do extraordinary things. (And he can use you, too.)

Remember, there are more than 3,400 personalities mentioned in the Old and New Testament and Apocrypha. God would not have put them in there if they did not have something to teach us. Paul noted the wise advice and encouragement to be found in studying the Old Testament when he recorded in Romans 15:4, "For whatever was written in earlier times was written for our instruction, that through perseverance and the encouragement of the Scriptures we might have hope." (NASB)

> God uses nobodies and turns them into somebodies.

God's inspired writers remind us time and time again that we all need encouragement. We all need hope. We all need tranquility and peace of mind. We all need to seek wisdom. We all need to connect with wise, inspiring believers.

The award-winning writer David Aikman notes the importance of inspiring people (souls) when he wrote in his book *Great Souls*, "I have always personally been inspired by the lives of great people. It is hard not to be energized by the stories of how individuals have risen above adversity or suffering, or have maintained a purity in the face of great temptation." (So true.)

> "It is never too late to become the person you could have been."
>
> Pen Name George Eliot
> Mary Anne Evans (1819-1880)

**Let me challenge you
to become one of those great souls that
God would be proud of.**

I pray and hope that the words in this book
can help you do this.
(I am also praying for myself.)

AN INTRODUCTION TO KIPLING

The Spiritual Hall of Fame

Another way that I have learned to help wisdom seekers acquire the behaviors and virtues found in this soul-changing poem is to have them create a Spiritual Hall of Fame.* (This will inspire you!)

To help you find nominees for your Hall of Fame, I challenge you to look for those individuals, not only in Scripture, but those you meet in everyday life, who exemplify the Christlike virtues and behaviors that Kipling so succinctly describes in "If," and ask what you can learn from them. The key question would be: Would **you** induct **yourself** into your own Spiritual Hall of Fame? And if not, why not?

> When you feel discouraged, seek out encouragement.

<u>Validations</u>

In 2002, I wrote a draft of my ideas for this book. This draft was used quite successfully as a pilot project and devotional guide in a Sunday School class to see if it would enhance, invigorate, and complement their Bible study. The leader of the class assured me that it did. She noted that every time they met they brought their nominees for their Spiritual Hall of Fame, placed them on a bulletin board, and entered into a lively discussion about what they could learn from each example as it related to a specific virtue in "If" and related Scriptures. She told me that some class members memorized the poem and

---

* I included this idea in my book *Lessons Learned from Kipling's "If"* (2000) and in my revised edition *A Unique Look at Kipling's Poem "If"* (2013). I also fantasized and created "The Over-comer Club."

felt inspired by this accomplishment. (You would be too!)

I was also humbled and honored to receive a testimony from a former newspaper editor who changed jobs after he read a draft of this book. My son-in-law, Todd Fox, had given him a copy. After he read Chapter 11, where I discussed Kipling's thoughts on risk taking, he decided to make a lifestyle change.

I called him and he told me about his decision and invited me to lunch with him the next time I visited in his area. When I finally had the opportunity to meet with him, he told me that my book stirred him to reassess where he was in life personally and professionally. He said he was especially influenced by the Scripture in Deuteronomy 1:6-8 where the writer states,

> What Scriptures influence or inspire you? Why?

"You have stayed here long enough on this mountain: move on." (MSG) He said that he had been contemplating a professional change for quite some time, and this particular verse and Kipling's wise advice catapulted him into quitting his job at the newspaper to follow his dream to become a full-time golf teacher.

I highlight this testimony, not to puff myself up, but to remind you again to seek out the wisdom found from wise people, the Bible, and "If," when you feel you need some encouragement or guidance about your purpose in life or some changes you feel you need to make.

> "All things desirable to men are contained in the Bible."
> Abraham Lincoln

§§§

Along with Kipling, another one of my favorite

poets is Emily Dickinson. This inspired and empathetic poet had just one of her hundreds of poems published during her lifetime. I wanted to include her poem, "If I Can Stop One Heart from Breaking," in this book because it touches a spiritual nerve in me and reminds me that one person can make a difference. Reflect upon her compassionate sentiments:

> If I can stop <u>one</u> heart from breaking,
> I shall not live in vain;
>
> If I can ease <u>one</u> life the aching,
> Or cool one pain,
>
> Or help <u>one</u> fainting robin
> Unto his nest again,
>
> I shall not live in vain.
> (emphasis mine)

> Emily reminds us (as does God) that acts of compassion can add meaning to our lives.

Emily may have had God in mind when she wrote these inspired words, for God reminds us time and time again in the Scriptures to be compassionate and considerate of others. He also challenges us to advocate and speak up for those who may falter or need a helping hand. As Paul reminds us in Romans 15:1, "Those of us who are strong and able in the faith need to step in and lend a hand to those who falter, and not just do what is most convenient for us. Strength is for service, not status. Each one of us needs to look

> **The Golden Rule**
> "Do to others as you would have them do to you."
> Luke 6:31 (NIV)
> (Do you practice this every day?)

after the good of the people around us, asking ourselves, **'How can I help?'** That's exactly what Jesus did." (MSG, emphasis mine) Peter echoed these sentiments when he noted in Acts 10:38 that Jesus came to do good.

> Jesus came to do good. What are you here for?

I know God would be proud of you and me if we just tried to help that one Robin, that one person we encounter who may need a little help, encouragement, or pat on the back.

In sum, if I can help just one robin unto his nest again, I will feel that this book has not been written in vain.

> Powerful Insight:
>
> "The printed page and the Godly life are the two most powerful tools of evangelism."
>
> Dr. Charles R. Swindoll, *The Darkness and the Dawn*

Have you found your **Robin** for today?

AN INTRODUCTION TO KIPLING

A Confession and Concern

Before we get to Kipling's poem "If" and my commentary, I want to confess to you right up front that I cannot always do what I know God or Kipling would want me to do, but I am trying. Paul, in his great honesty, reminds us in Romans 7:15-20 that he also struggled with doing what he knew he should do. So did Peter and David. (Luke 5:8, 1 Chronicles 21:8)

> Paul said:
> "I decide to do good, but I don't really do it; I decide not to do bad, but then I do it anyway."
> Romans 7:19 (MSG)

I also tend to be a little suspicious of people who claim to be great Christians but whose deeds and actions don't match their words. Sadly, history reminds us that some people are not who they want us to believe they are. The writer of the book of James notes that faith without actions is no faith. He said, "What good is it, my brothers, if a man claims to have faith but has no deeds?" (James 2:14 NIV) James reminds us that if your faith is real and genuine, it will inevitably show in your actions. Nearly a thousand years ago, Saint Francis of Assissi echoed James' insight with this powerful challenge:

> Beware of false prophets, which come to you in sheep's clothing, but inwardly they are ravening wolves.
> Matthew 7:15 (KJV)

"Preach the gospel at all times.
If necessary, use words."

Of course, words are important – they can heal us or hurt us, but what a person actually does often reveals his or her true character.

Another Challenge

If you find some Biblical or secular personality who reflects a virtue in "If" that excites or interests you, I challenge you to find out more about them. Google them or go to the library and find out about them. Seek out Biblical scholars and other learned people who can enlighten you about your questions or concerns.

§§§

Be open to the fact that God may use unusual methods to speak to your heart, such as a friend, minister, stranger, book, or even a poem. For example, Philip Yancey, the insightful, award-winning spiritual writer,

> Maybe God will allow you to see a poem, a book, a work of art, or a spiritual symbol illuminated in a different way.

noted in his book *The Jesus I Never Knew* that he gained greater understanding about "The Sermon on the Mount" after reading novels written by Tolstoy and Dostoevsky. And, as I have noted, God has used Kipling's "If" to help me and countless others acquire the behaviors and virtues that I believe would please Him.

§§§

Remember, my goal in this book is not to go into depth with any of the Biblical examples I have used, but to highlight some of their behavioral characteristics as they relate to the wisdom found in "If." Hopefully, the Biblical personalities I have focused on, plus the wisdom found in "If" and the related wisdom-filled Scriptures, will speak to your heart and propel you to think about your spirituality, thoughts, values, behaviors, and concerns.

"He who walks with the wise grows wise ..."
Proverbs 13:20 (NIV)

Now, let us go walk and talk with
some wise men and women from the Bible.

With God's help, I will work on acquiring and developing these personality traits.

Stanza One

If you can keep your head when all about you
Are losing theirs and blaming it on you;
If you can trust yourself when all men doubt you,
But make allowance for their doubting too:
If you can wait and not be tired by waiting,
Or, being lied about, don't deal in lies,
Or, being hated, don't give way to hating,
And yet don't look too good, nor talk too wise;

Have you memorized this character-building stanza?

Chapter 1
"If you can keep your head when all about you are losing theirs and blaming it on you;"

Moses could. Can you?
Books of Exodus and Numbers

If you have ever been in a leadership position, or for that matter, in any meaningful relationship, you have probably experienced situations in which you were blamed for certain negative circumstances or outcomes that you had no control over. Moses was.

Here is the scenario.

After Moses spent 40 long years in the desert as a shepherd nobody, God knocked him out of his comfort zone and charged him with the responsibility of leading His (God's) people out of Egyptian slavery. This request surprised and confused Moses because he did not feel qualified to do it. He said in Exodus 4:13, "Lord, please! send someone else." (NIV) But, Moses was to learn that when God calls you, you had better listen. Remember, if God calls you and you do what he asks you to do, he will prepare you and be with you every step of the way. (Hebrews 13:21, Exodus 4:12)

> "... I will help you speak and will teach you what to say."
> God speaking to Moses
> Exodus 4:12

After some prodding, Moses did what God told him. He went to Egypt and tried to reason with the Pharaoh. After negotiations failed, God had to send 10 terrible plagues to get the stubborn Pharaoh's attention.

It did, and he finally consented to let God's people go. Things were proceeding fairly well for the Jewish slaves, until the fickle Pharaoh had a change of heart. He broke his promise. He wanted his slaves returned and sent his soldiers in their chariots after them. When the slaves saw the Egyptian army coming, they became scared and lost faith in Moses' leadership. They turned against Moses and blamed him for their situation. (It would seem there are always people looking to blame others for their predicament.)

> Since Moses represented God, the slaves, in effect, were blaming Him for their condition.

And because of the slaves' fear of the Egyptian army and their distorted thinking about Moses, they devised a plan to stone and kill him. They felt they would be better off returning to Egypt as slaves than to be massacred in the desert. (Their attitude reminds us that sometimes the unknown is scarier than the known, even if the known is unbearable.)

But, with God's help, Moses got control of the situation, kept his head, and assured the slaves that God would not forsake them. And that everything would be okay if they kept their faith. In essence, the Lord would help them fight their battles. (Aren't we glad that we have someone to help us fight our battles?) Thus, Moses encouraged his people to hang on, trust God, and believe in his leadership.

After Moses got his people recharged and refocused, he was able to lead them toward the Promised Land by way of the Red Sea. As they approached the sea, God performed a miracle. He told Moses to point his shepherd's staff toward the water and a path would open up so they could cross on dry ground. As God had

CHAPTER 1: IF YOU CAN KEEP YOUR HEAD...

promised, the waters parted and the slaves were able to safely cross to the other side. When the Pharaoh's soldiers tried to follow, the wheels fell off their chariots and the waters came back together, drowning them. This all happened because Moses did not panic, kept his head, and did what God commanded him to do.

Remember, Moses was not insensitive to the slaves' lack of faith, and he could see how they could be scared and blame him for what they perceived as an impossible situation to get out of. But, Moses reminded the slaves, and he reminds us today, that with God's help we can overcome whatever situation or circumstance the enemy sends our way.

Moses also reassures us that God can use us no matter what our flaws or weaknesses. Keep in mind, Moses lived with self-doubt, inner turmoil, and a speech impediment.

In addition, he had a violent temper. For example, when he was a young, arrogant, 40-year-old Egyptian prince, he became so angry when he witnessed an Egyptian beating a Jewish slave that he killed the Egyptian and buried his body. When the Pharaoh found out about it, Moses had to flee for his life. You might say at this point in Moses' life that he temporarily lost his head.

> Remember: Samson self-destructed because of his lack of self-control.
> Judges 16

Moses reminds us that keeping one's head (maintaining self-control) is not always easy to do, especially if we are outside of God's will. And because of Moses' lack of self control, fiery attitude, and arrogance, God decided to send him to the desert for 40 long years for some attitude retraining and to help him acquire some humility and maturity. Interestingly, God decided to use Moses' wise father-in-law to help him learn how to control his anger and emotions.

> Ask God to send someone into your life who can help you control your emotions.

The Bible suggests that Moses would need all of his acquired wisdom and maturity to lead the rebellious and ungrateful Israelites toward the Promised Land. (Modern day Israel.) For the Bible records that when the Israelites finally approached their future home, they again showed their lack of faith when scouts reported that there were giants waiting there to harm them.

This report so unnerved the former slaves that they became afraid and did not want to follow God's instructions. Because of their rebellion, cowardice and lack of faith, God decided not to allow the adults to enter into the land He promised them. And for their rebelliousness, He made them wander in the desert for 40 years until all the adults died off. He then allowed the second generation of Israelites to proceed to their future home.

> Figuratively Speaking:
> What giants are you afraid of?

Because of the former slaves' constant griping and complaining, the Bible records that Moses often became despondent and depressed. After one severe bout of depression, he even asked God to kill him. (Numbers 11:15) God heard Moses' cry for help, and He reached down and renewed him with hope and a plan that would help him lead the Israelites toward their destiny.

> When you feel dejected or depressed, look up, pray up, and ask God to give you some relief as He did for Moses.

In essence, Moses reminds us that with God's help anything is possible. He also reminds us that with faith and

CHAPTER 1: IF YOU CAN KEEP YOUR HEAD...

desire we can learn to keep our heads (self-control) when facing a crisis or difficult time. Moses also teaches us that even though we can't always control our circumstances, we can control how we will react to them. Ask God to help you react appropriately to your circumstances.

Remember, God wants us to be the master of our emotions. He wants us to lean on Him in our times of need. He wants us to keep our heads.

**"If you can keep your head when all about you
Are losing theirs and blaming it on you;"**

SOMETHING TO PONDER
Remember, Moses was 80 years old when God called him to lead His people to the Promised Land. He reminds us that we are never too old to answer God's call. (Seniors, don't give up.)

THE SPIRITUAL WISDOM OF IF

"If you can keep your head when all about you
Are losing theirs and blaming it on you;"

§§§

Meditate on These Related Wisdom-Filled Scriptures

"A person without self-control is like a house with its doors and windows knocked out."
Proverbs 25:21 (MSG)

"…it is better to have self-control than to control an army."
Proverbs 17:32 (TLB)

"Therefore…be self-controlled."
1 Peter 1:13 (NIV)

How can you apply these Scriptures to your life?

CHAPTER 1: IF YOU CAN KEEP YOUR HEAD...

Remember, With God's Help:

§§§

- I will not let other people's attitudes and outlooks determine mine.
- I will not become negative when negative things are said about me.
- I will react the way God leads me to react.
- I can function where there is disorder.
- I will keep my head when others are losing theirs.

Remember to pray …
Dear God, as you did for Moses, give me the wisdom and the help I need to control my emotions and give me the courage to do what is right in your eyes.

**"If you can keep your head when all about you
Are losing theirs and blaming it on you;"**

What did you learn from this chapter?

Chapter 2

"If you can trust yourself when all men doubt you, But make allowance for their doubting too:"

Daniel could. Can you?
Book of Daniel

It is hard to trust and believe in yourself when you are surrounded by people who want to confuse you or push you into doing something that you know is wrong and that would displease God. Daniel understood how hard it is to stand up and trust yourself and do the right thing. For he was challenged and tested many times in his life to do the things he knew were morally and spiritually wrong. But he reminds us that with God's help, we can stand up to those who are trying to lead us astray. Here is the abbreviated story of Daniel's challenges in relation to Kipling's couplet.

Around 600 B.C. the Kingdom of Judah was captured by the Babylonian ruler Nebuchadnezzar. After the Babylonians had captured a country, it was their practice to round up the wisest, smartest, and most competent young men, send them to Babylon, and train them to serve in the king's palace. Because of his talents and remarkable people skills, Daniel was one of those chosen.

The Bible records that Daniel was an excellent manager and confidante to the four kings he served under. He was also a devoutly faithful man of God, and never forgot to thank God for his unusual gifts. But, there were

CHAPTER 2: IF YOU CAN TRUST YOURSELF...

some things he just would not do. For example: Daniel would not eat meat because he was a vegetarian nor anything from the king's table. And he would not worship false idols even though he was pressured to do so. His stubbornness and peculiarities offended many people.

> "He gives wisdom to the wise and knowledge to the discerning ... I thank and praise you, O god of my fathers: You have given me wisdom and power ..."
>
> Daniel 2:21-23 (NIV)

When Daniel was about 80 and still going strong, Darius the Mede conquered the Babylonians. Daniel got along well with Darius; actually, he got along too well. Because of his favor with the king and his independent spirit, certain members of the royal court became extremely jealous of Daniel. (Jealousy is a powerful and detrimental emotion).

Darius liked Daniel and knew he was a man of faith and was honorable. He also knew that Daniel was a wise, loyal, and competent government official. But, because Daniel would not conform to the Babylonians' customs or give up his prayer life and worship like them, Daniel's enemies hatched a plot against him and talked the king into throwing him into the lions' den to die.

> Remember:
> Prayer is your lifeline to God.

The Bible records that Daniel was willing to die for his beliefs. In effect, he said, "I am not changing; bring on the lions." Daniel also had sympathy for Darius, who he knew was basically a decent man, and Daniel understood the predicament he put the king in with his behaviors.

Technically, Darius understood that Daniel was guilty as charged, but he had mixed feelings about what to do. On the one hand, he hated to go against his advisors, who wanted Daniel killed, but he also did not believe Daniel deserved the death penalty. Because of his uncertainty and anguish about what

> Be leery of people who seem to have no conscience.

to do, his conscience began to bother him. He became so confused and distraught about placing Daniel in the lions' den that it affected his sleep and he spent nights fasting and worrying. He knew he had made a mistake. But he did not have the courage to stand up against the members of his royal court. (Do you have the courage to stand up when you need to stand up?)

Because of God's intervention, the story of Daniel in the lions' den has a happy ending. For the Bible notes that "God sent his angel and shut the lions' mouths" (Daniel 6:22 RSV). Thus, Daniel's life was saved. This miracle served as a wake up call for Darius and moved him to repent and become a true believer.

> Do you need a wake up call in order to do what you know you should do?

Daniel reminds us that the secular world will often try to conform us and bend us to its ways, but he also reminds us that with God's help we can find the encouragement to trust our better instincts and resist those who would harm us and try to lead us astray.

**"If you can trust yourself when all men doubt you,
But make allowance for their doubting too:"**

CHAPTER 2: IF YOU CAN TRUST YOURSELF...

"If you can trust yourself when all men doubt you,
But make allowance for their doubting too:"

§§§

Meditate on These Related Wisdom-Filled Scriptures

"Anyone who trusts in Him will never be put to shame."
Romans 10:11 (NIV)

"Trust in the Lord with all your heart and lean not on your own understanding; in all your ways acknowledge him, and he will make your paths straight."
Proverbs 3:5-6 (NIV)

"The Lord is good, a refuge in times of trouble. He cares for those who trust in him."
Nahum 1:7 (NIV)

How can you apply these Scriptures to your life?

Remember, With God's Help:

§§§

- I will trust in myself after seeking God's wisdom concerning my situation.
- I will do what I know God would want me to do.
- I will trust in God's Word and promises when surrounded by nonbelievers.

Remember to pray …
Dear God, just as you did for Daniel, give me the strength, wisdom, and courage to do the right thing when I am faced with uncertainty and adversity.

**"If you can trust yourself when all men doubt you,
But make allowance for their doubting too:"**

What did you learn from this chapter?

Chapter 3
"If you can wait and not be tired by waiting,"

Jacob could. Can you?
Book of Genesis

Waiting and patience are not two of my stronger virtues. Nor would it appear from observing human nature that waiting and patience are virtues that most of us possess.

Jacob, though, reminds us that some things are worth waiting for, sacrificing for. But he did not gain this insight overnight; he had some help from God. For you see, Jacob, being human, sinned and would later suffer the consequences of his actions.

> "For ye have need of patience."
> (Hebrews 10:36, KJV)

And what was this sin? It was the sin of lying and distorting the truth so he could acquire something that he did not earn. Basically, with his unscrupulous and biased mother's help, he fooled his dying and confused father, Isaac, into believing he was his older brother. By doing this, he won the birthright that goes to the first-born son, which gave him all of the privileges of inheritance.

But, as the Bible reminds us, we reap what we sow. When Esau found out about Jacob's dishonesty and greed, he set out to kill him. After Jacob's mother Rebekah found out about Esau's intentions, she begged Isaac to let her send Jacob, her favorite son, to live with her brother Laban in Haran, a place where she had grown up and where she felt he would be safe. Isaac honored Rebekah's request.

While in Haran, Jacob ran into his beautiful cousin Rachel. The Bible records that he immediately fell in love with her. The chemistry was there. It was love at first sight. (Keep in mind, at this time people could intermarry.) Laban, Rachel's father, agreed to let Jacob marry her, but only after Jacob offered to work for him for seven years. Talk about a commitment. Talk about waiting. Talk about true love.

> "So Jacob served seven years to get Rachel, but they seemed like only a few days to him because of his love for her."
>
> (Genesis 29:30, NIV)

Jacob could have said, "There is no way I'm going to wait seven long years to marry anyone. I'll just find someone else." But hang on. This story gets even better.

The writer of Genesis notes that uncle Laban was a dishonest and conniving character who was about to teach Jacob a thing or two about dishonesty and waiting. For the Bible records that when the seven years were up, Laban had another trick up his sleeve. And this was to trick Jacob into marrying Rachel's older and less-attractive sister, Leah. (Of course, we know that

> "Do not be deceived, God is not mocked; for whatever a man sows, this he will also reap."
>
> (Galatians 6:7, NASB)

Jacob brought much of his misery on himself by his earlier dishonesty). Even though Jacob cared for Leah, his heart was with Rachel. The Bible records that he was able to marry Rachel a week after marrying Leah, but in order to do this, he had to agree to work seven more years as an indentured servant for uncle Laban. Think about this. Fourteen years he had to work for Laban before he could take Rachel and head for home.

> "Patience is the companion of wisdom."
>
> St. Augustine

With the help of maturity

CHAPTER 3: IF YOU CAN WAIT AND NOT BE TIRED...

and reflection, Jacob wisely began to realize that some things are worth waiting for. And he was willing to wait and wait for his true love! Are you willing to wait?

In essence, Jacob reminds us of the importance of developing patience and waiting for that something (degree, house, money, cars) or that someone (marriage) God has in mind for us. He also reminds us of the importance of deferred gratification and the importance of learning how to wait without becoming frustrated. (As Kipling would say, these are signs of maturity.)

In sum, when you are down and out and feel lost and you think God has forgotten about your troubles, just remember that God uses a different time schedule and a different clock than we do.

> "But they that wait upon the Lord shall renew their strengths; they shall mount up with wings as eagles; they shall run, and not be weary; and they shall walk, and not faint."
>
> (Isaiah 40:31, KJV)

Thus, our timing may not God's timing. But never doubt that those who wait upon the Lord will win in the end.

"If you can wait and not be tired by waiting,"

THE SPIRITUAL WISDOM OF IF
"If you can wait and not be tired by waiting,"

§§§

Meditate on These Related Wisdom-Filled Scriptures

"But if we hope for that which we see not, then do we with patience wait for it."
Romans 8:25 (KJV)

"There is a time for everything, and a season for every activity under heaven."
Ecclesiastes 3:1 (NIV)

"Wait on the Lord: be of good courage and he shall strengthen thine heart: wait, I say, on the Lord."
Psalms 27:14 (KJV)

"Better a patient man than a warrior …"
Proverbs 16:32 (NIV)

How can you apply these Scriptures to your life?

CHAPTER 3: IF YOU CAN WAIT AND NOT BE TIRED...

Remember, With God's Help:

§§§

- I will be sensitive to other people's schedules.
- I will develop patience and use it to my benefit rather than becoming frustrated and angry.
- I will remain calm when I am in a negative situation that I have no control over.

Remember to pray …
Dear God, give me the wisdom and the ability to develop patience as you did for Jacob.

"If you can wait and not be tired by waiting,"

What did you learn from this chapter?

Chapter 4

"Or, being lied about, don't deal in lies,"

Stephen was lied about, but he didn't deal in lies.
Can you do this?
Book of Acts

Who was Stephen? What was his situation? Why was he described as the first martyr in the Bible? What can we learn from him as it relates to Kipling's thoughts on lying? Let's find out.

Luke records that Stephen was a passionate speaker and debater who was filled with the Holy Spirit and considered a leader among his people. (Acts 6:3) And because of his wisdom, character, and reputation, he was one of seven chosen to manage the food program for the needy, which was considered a prestigious position during his lifetime.

Stephen was also highly ethical and could not tolerate liars and hypocrites. He especially could not tolerate the hypocrisy and deceitfulness of some of the Jewish leaders, and he often let them know about it. For example, he really upset them when he pointed out their dishonest and self-serving interpretations of Mosaic law and their failure to

> Hypocrite:
> a person who pretends to be what he is not; one who pretends to be better that he is, or to be pious, virtuous, etc. without really being so.
>
> Webster's New World Dictionary,
> 2nd College Edition

CHAPTER 4: BEING LIED ABOUT, DON'T DEAL IN LIES

obey God's laws: the very laws they pretended to follow. Stephen may have recalled Jesus's words, "practice what you preach," when he confronted the religious leaders about their hypocrisy (Matthew 23:3 NIV).

Luke said that they became so angry at Stephen for pointing out their dishonesty and hypocrisy that they gnashed their teeth and lost control of their senses. And they really became riled up when Stephen called them a stiff-necked people who had Jesus killed for their own selfish reasons. Because Stephen's enemies could not refute what the Holy Spirit had led him to say, some of them plotted to kill him. Their strategy was to find some evil men who would accuse him of spreading lies and innuendos. Their strategy worked and they were able to stir up the gullible masses against Stephen, which resulted in him being dragged out of town and stoned to death. What a horrible way to die! His accusers were not guided by God's motives, but by their own selfish agenda. (Sound familiar today?)

The Bible notes that one of those who agreed with the mob and cheered them on as they stoned Stephen was Saul of Tarsus, one mean individual who, at the time, was a great persecutor of Christians. I can just hear him shout, "Throw another stone." He would later convert to Christianity and become the great apostle Paul after his encounter with Jesus on the road to Damascus. (Don't tell me that God cannot transform people! From Christian-killer to Christian.)

Remember, young Stephen could have saved his life if he had apologized and agreed with his accusers, but he chose to stand up for what was right and tell the truth

> What would you be willing to die for? Is a long life always the best life?

as God had revealed it to him. Interestingly, the same accusations and lies that the accusers used against Stephen were the same lies used against Jesus.

As Stephen was dying, the Bible records that he saw a vision of heaven and a peace came over him. The Bible also notes that this courageous man spoke and died with a "glow."

> "Men, when you teach on heaven, let there always be a glow on your face, a gleam in your eye, and a grin on your lips."
> C.H. Spurgeon

Like Jesus, Stephen also had compassion for his enemies. Luke wrote that as he was being stoned he cried out, "Lord Jesus, receive my spirit ... do not hold this sin against them" (Acts 7:59-60 NKJV). Stephen was tough but tender. What a rare man!

Stephen's story and ultimate martyrdom reminds us that there will always be dishonest and evil people who will lie about someone or something to compensate for their own inadequacies, insecurities, or to move forward their own personal agenda. He reminds us that it often takes great courage to stand up for God and one's convictions when dealing with dishonest and hypocritical people, and that we may have to pay a big price to do it.

And finally, this fighter challenges us to forgive our enemies, as did Jesus. (The forgiving is hard enough for me, but the forgetting is even harder. What about you? Pray for me.)

"Or, being lied about, don't deal in lies,"

CHAPTER 4: BEING LIED ABOUT, DON'T DEAL IN LIES

"Or, being lied about, don't deal in lies,"

§§§

Meditate on These Related Wisdom-Filled Scriptures

"If you want a happy, good life, keep control of your tongue, and guard your lips from telling lies."
1 Peter 3:10 (TLB)

"Telling lies about others is as harmful as hitting them with an ax, wounding them with a sword, or shooting them with a sharp arrow."
Proverbs 25:18 (NLT)

"Just as damaging as a mad man shooting a lethal weapon is someone who lies to a friend and then says, 'I was just joking.'"
Proverbs 26:18 (NLT)

How can you apply these Scriptures to your life?

Remember, With God's Help:

§§§

- I will not lie.
- I won't seek revenge or become bitter when someone lies about me.

Remember to pray …
Dear God, give me the same courage to face
those who would lie about me as you did for
Stephen and give me the strength and wisdom to know
how to react to those who would harm me
with their slanderous words.

"Or, being lied about, don't deal in lies,"

What did you learn from this chapter?

Chapter 5
"Or, being hated, don't give way to hating,"

Joseph was hated, but he did not give in to hating. Can you do this?
Book of Genesis, See Chapter 37

Hate is such a strong emotion. None of us is free from those cruelties and evil deeds that could cause us to profoundly hate another person. But, we must be on guard against this strong emotion, because if we are not, it could consume and harm us in many ways. For example, hate could have ruined Joseph's life, but with God's help, it did not. Here is Joseph's story as it relates to Kipling's thought about hating.

For starters, the writer of Genesis notes that Joseph was deeply despised and was hated by his 10 older brothers because his father showed open favoritism to him. (Talk about poor parenting skills.) And because Joseph knew he was his father's favorite, he became a cocky smart-aleck teenager who did not show his brothers any respect. Because of his haughty attitude, his jealous brothers conspired to kill him. But, at the last moment, his brother Reuben talked them out of it, and they decided to sell him to slave-traders, who hauled him to Egypt.

While he was in servitude in Egypt, he became the property of a powerful captain in the Egyptian army whose name was Potiphar. Potiphar recognized Joseph's talents and put him in charge of his household. (Quite a prestigious assignment for a slave.)

The Bible records that Joseph was also blessed with good looks. And Potiphar's conniving wife noticed this and tried to seduce him. But Joseph would not give in to her no matter how enticing she made the offer. He would not commit adultery, nor would he violate the trust that Potiphar had shown him. (What a model of integrity!) But, Potiphar's wife would not give up. One day she caught him in what she thought was a vulnerable situation. She literally grabbed at him, and when he fled from her, he accidentally left his coat behind. She was so incensed by his rejection of her that she screamed and yelled so loudly that the servants rushed to see what had happened. She lied to them and said that Joseph had tried to rape her. She later told her husband the same false story. For some reason, he did not have Joseph killed. Instead, he had him locked up in the royal prison for two years. Joseph was punished for trying to do the right thing. (Sadly, Joseph's story sometimes reminds us of the negative phrase that "no good deed goes unpunished.")

Think about all the reasons Joseph had to hate: sold into slavery by his brothers; cast into prison because of a jealous, evil woman; and unjustly imprisoned for 13 long years. How many of us could be imprisoned this length of time for crimes we did not commit and not feel bitter and harbor anger and hatred for those who put us into the situation?

But, with spiritual growth and maturity, Joseph was able to keep his life in perspective and his anger in check. And with God's nudging he was able to come to peace with his past and forgive his brothers for the harm they did to him.

Because of his abilities and faith, the Bible records

CHAPTER 5: BEING HATED, DON'T GIVE WAY TO HATING

that Joseph eventually became the most powerful government official in Pharaoh's court. This nobody became, in essence, the prime minister of Egypt. (Wow! From prison to prime minister.) Joseph reminds us that with God's help, one can endure hardships and setbacks. He also reminds us, as did Stephen, that God wants us to develop the spirit of forgiveness.

> ... I have learned that no one can experience true love or a joyful presence or create an optimal future until he or she makes peace with the past. ...
>
> from *Making Peace With Your Past* by Dr. Harold H. Bloomfield

"Or, being hated, don't give way to hating,"

> REMEMBER:
> WHEN FACING ADVERSITY ...
>
> STAND UP, LOOK UP, HOOK UP,
>
> AND
> WITH GOD'S HELP
> DON'T GIVE UP!

THE SPIRITUAL WISDOM OF IF
"Or, being hated, don't give way to hating,"

§§§

Meditate on These Related Wisdom-Filled Scriptures

"Do not let the sun go down while you are still angry."
Ephesians 4:26 (NIV)

"My dear brothers, take note of this: Everyone should be quick to listen, slow to speak and slow to become angry, for a man's anger does not bring about the righteous life that God desires."
James 1:19-20 (NIV)

"You have heard that it was said, 'Eye for eye, and tooth for tooth.' But I tell you, Do not resist an evil person. If someone strikes you on the right cheek, I turn to him the other also."
Matthew 5:38-39 (NIV)

"Beloved, never avenge yourselves, but leave it to the wrath of God; for it is written, 'Vengeance is mine, I will repay, says the Lord.'"
Romans 12:19 (RSV)

"Do not repay anyone evil for evil. Be careful to do what is right in the eyes of everybody. If it is possible, as far as it depends on you, live at peace with everybody."
Romans 12: 17-18 (NIV)

"Then Peter came up and said to him, 'Lord, how often

CHAPTER 5: BEING HATED, DON'T GIVE WAY TO HATING

shall my brother sin against me, and I forgive him? As many as seven times?' Jesus said unto him, 'I do not say to you seven times, but seventy times seven.'"
Matthew 18:21-22 (RSV)

How can you apply these Scriptures to your life?

Remember, With God's Help:

§§§

- I will not take out my anger on those who love me and care for me when I have been angered by others.
- I will not let hatred destroy my life.
- I will find a positive outlet for my anger.

Remember to pray …
Dear God, as you did for Joseph, give me the ability and strength to move on with my life when I have been harmed by others who seem to hate me. And give me the compassion to not hate those who hate me.

"Or, being hated, don't give way to hating,"

What did you learn from this chapter?

Chapter 6
"And yet don't look too good, or talk too wise;"

David and Abigail understood the wisdom in this virtue.
Do you?
Book of 1 Samuel

David was confident, but never arrogant or pretentious. He never pretended to be something he wasn't. Even when Samuel anointed him with oil, which signaled to him and to the rest of the Israelites that he was to eventually replace Saul as the new king, he never shouted, "Look at me, I'm the new king; everybody bow down." No, he went back to tending his flock of sheep and waited upon the Lord to elevate him to the kingship.

> "Let someone else praise you,
> not your own mouth –
> a stranger,
> not your own lips."
> Proverbs 27:2 (NLT)

The Bible records that David also knew when to be prudent (or wise) in speech and when to control his tongue and use the right phrase. As Samuel says in 1 Samuel 16:18, "I have seen a son of Jesse the Bethlehemite (David) who is a skillful musician, a mighty man of valor, a warrior, one **prudent** in speech, and a handsome man; and the Lord is with him." (NASB, emphasis mine)

Although David knew he was going to eventually replace Saul as king of Israel, he never once tried to upstage King Saul or belittle him. He was never jealous of Saul's position. The Bible notes that he was subservient enough to serve as Saul's armor bearer and even consented to play the harp for Saul when the king was suffering from severe depression. David was definitely not a show-off or a pop-off, and neither was his future wife Abigail.

Abigail was an unusually gifted and outgoing person who was married to an abusive man named Nabal. Nabal was a wealthy and mean-spirited herder who managed to insult David, and David was out for revenge. David, being a man with great strengths and great flaws, momentarily lost his mind when he became so mad at this slight from Nabal that he and his 400 men went after him with the thought of killing him and his household. But the Bible records that God used Abigail as a mediator to change David's mind. Keep in mind that Abigail took a great risk in acting as a mediator, because she knew her husband would not approve of her decision to try to diffuse the situation, even though she was doing it to keep him alive.

Now the question is, how did this remarkable woman keep David and his men from killing her entire household? Because she had a God-inspired plan. But before she could implement her plan she had to get David and his men's attention. As described in 1 Samuel 25:18-19, she did this by preparing a big meal for them. (Nothing will get a man's attention more than a bountiful meal if he is hungry, especially if it is served by a charming/pleasant woman.)

The Bible goes on to record that after she got David's attention with the meal, she was able to change his mind because of her demeanor, sincerity, humility, and choice of words. **(In essence, she knew when not to look too good or talk too wise.)** Some people call this tact. For example, we find in 1 Samuel (NASB), that she

CHAPTER 6: AND YET DON'T LOOK TOO GOOD...

referred to herself as "your maidservant," and eight times she called David "my lord." She showed him great respect. As the insightful writer Charles Swindoll pointed out in his book about David, Abigail "is a study in wisdom."

Because of Abigail's tact, (what a powerful personality trait to possess) she definitely saved David from making a huge mistake. She had the persona and the ability to persuade and figuratively reach into David's heart and remind David that, "Vengeance is mine, says the Lord." Abigail reminds us that a wise person knows when to speak the right words. (Can you do this?)

> "Everyone enjoys a fitting reply; it is wonderful to say the right things at the right time!"
> Proverbs 15:23 (NLT)

As I have noted, Nabal did not appreciate what Abigail did to save his life. And because of her efforts, he became so enraged that he had a stroke and later died. (Resentment and anger can ruin your health.) When David found out that Nabal had died, he remembered Abigail's advice in encouraging him not to kill her husband, and because of his respect for her, he took her as his wife.

David and Abigail remind us that God is offended by pretentious and vain behavior. They also remind us that with God, character counts, and that what we say and how we say it matters. As Solomon reminds us, "Wise words satisfy like a good meal; the right words bring satisfaction" (Proverbs 18:20 NLT). So true.

"And yet don't look too good, or talk too wise;"

THE SPIRITUAL WISDOM OF IF

"And yet don't look too good, or talk too wise;"

§§§

Meditate on These Related Wisdom-Filled Scriptures

"Do not look on his appearance or on the height of his stature, because I have rejected him; for the Lord sees not as man sees; man looks on the outward appearance, but the Lord looks on the heart."
1 Samuel 16:7 (RSV)

"God can't stomach arrogance or pretense;
believe me, he'll put those upstarts in their place."
Proverbs 16:5 (MSG)

"Do you see a man wise in his own eyes? There is more hope for a fool than for him."
Proverbs 26:12 (NIV)

"The mouths of fools are their ruin; their lips get them into trouble."
Proverbs 18:7 (NLT)

"Don't call attention to yourself; let others do that for you."
Proverbs 27:19 (MSG)

"The tongue can bring death or life; those who love to talk will reap the consequences."
Proverbs 18:21 (NLT)

"When pride comes, then comes disgrace,

CHAPTER 6: AND YET DON'T LOOK TOO GOOD...
but with humility comes wisdom."
Proverbs 11:2 (NIV)

"Blessed are the meek, for they will inherit the earth."
Matthew 5:5 (NIV)

How can you apply these Scriptures to your life?

Remember, With God's Help:

§§§

- I will be confident, but not arrogant or self-serving.
- I will develop the ability to communicate with all kinds of people.
- I will not be showy or pretentious.

Remember to pray …
Dear God, help me to be humble and void of all arrogance, as were David and Abigail.

"And yet don't look too good, or talk too wise;"

What did you learn from this chapter?

With God's help I will work on acquiring
and developing these personality traits.

Stanza Two

If you can dream – and not make dreams your master;
If you can think – and not make thoughts your aim,
If you can meet with Triumph and Disaster
And treat those two impostors just the same:
If you can bear to hear the truth you've spoken
Twisted by knaves to make a trap for fools,
Or watch the things you gave your life to, broken,
And stoop and build'em up with worn-out tools;

Have you memorized this character-building stanza?

Chapter 7
"If you can dream – and not make dreams your master;
If you can think – and not make thoughts your aim."

Nehemiah could. Can you?
Book of Nehemiah

Nehemiah was a devout man of prayer and action. He also had a burning dream (goal). His dream was to motivate and encourage his demoralized kinsmen in Jerusalem to take back control of their city from their enemies and rebuild the wall that surrounded it. And with God's nudging and help, he developed a plan of action to accomplish what his heart told him to do.

> Have you turned your dreams and thoughts into reality? If not, why not?

> Do you have a workable plan to help you aquire what your heart tells you to do.

Here is Nehemiah's abbreviated story.

The Bible notes that he was a cupbearer for King Artaxerxes of Persia, which meant he tasted the wine and food before it was given to the king to make sure it wasn't poisoned. (Talk about a tough job.) Because Nehemiah was a good and faithful servant and a diligent cupbearer, he became one of the king's favorites. And for this he was rewarded with a very comfortable and secure lifestyle.

But this well to do lifestyle did not keep him from becoming depressed; a depression so severe and obvious that the king noticed it and asked Nehemiah what was wrong. Nehemiah explained to the king that Jerusalem,

CHAPTER 7: IF YOU CAN DREAM...

the town that he was raised in, had been ravaged and the wall that protected it was destroyed.

The Bible notes that Nehemiah was so distressed upon finding out about the condition of his hometown that he wept uncontrollably and had trouble functioning. His internalized pain eventually began to show in his countenance and outlook on life. Because the king thought so much of Nehemiah, he wanted to know what he could do to help ease his distress. Nehemiah told the king about his burning desire to rebuild the wall. After some reflection, he boldly asked the king for permission to rebuild it. The king granted his request.

As you might expect, Nehemiah's efforts to turn his God-given dream into a reality did not come without great effort and struggle. For the Bible notes that the governors from the outlying empires were jealous of Nehemiah and did not want him to accomplish his dream of restoring the wall that surrounded Jerusalem. These bad men tried all sorts of evil ways to keep him from being successful. They even attempted to kill him on several occasions. But because of Nehemiah's determination to do what God had planted in his mind and soul, he would not be deterred by his enemies or anything else. And because of his tenacity, skills, and God's favor, he accomplished his goal of completing and restoring the wall around his beloved city in an impressive 52 days.

Nehemiah reminds us that we need a reason to live. We need a reason to get up in the morning and be excited about life. Solomon understood this. He wrote, "Where there is no vision, the people perish" (Proverbs 29:18 KJV).

> When was the last time you were passionate about something?

(If you are not passionate about something, look

up and ask God for help.)

Nehemiah reminds us that with God on our side and a plan of action our dreams can come true. As Solomon said in Proverbs 16:3, "Put God in charge of your work (your dreams, your thoughts) then what you've planned will take place." (MSG, emphasis mine)

> **A Thought:**
> Remember, if you are mismatched, miscast, or misaligned in a relationship or in your job, you can function, but you will never be truly happy or be the person you were designed to be.

"If you can dream – and not make dreams your master;
If you can think – and not make thoughts your aim."

CHAPTER 7: IF YOU CAN DREAM...

"If you can dream – and not make dreams your master;
If you can think – and not make thoughts your aim."

§§§

Meditate on These Related Wisdom-Filled Scriptures

"In all thy ways acknowledge him, and he shall direct thy paths."
Proverbs 3:6 (KJV)

"Dreaming instead of doing is foolishness …"
Ecclesiastes 5:7 (TLB)

"… mere dreaming of nice things is foolish; it's chasing the wind."
Ecclesiastes 6:9 (TLB)

"Hope deferred makes the heart sick … but when dreams come true at last, there is life and joy."
Proverbs 13:12 (TLB)

How can you apply these Scriptures to your life?

Remember, With God's Help:

§§§

- I can turn my dreams and thoughts into realities.
- I can accomplish what I set out to do.

Remember to pray …
Dear God, as you did for Nehemiah, help me to find and pursue my purpose in life. And then give me the courage to do what you called me to do.

"If you can dream – and not make dreams your master;
If you can think – and not make thoughts your aim."

What did you learn from this chapter?

Chapter 8
"If you can meet with Triumph and Disaster And treat those two impostors just the same:"

Paul could. Can you?
Books of Acts and Philippians

Next to Jesus, there was probably nobody in the New Testament more exalted and revered than Paul, nor conversely more despised or hated. And nobody, except Jesus, probably knew more about triumph and disaster than Paul.

Luke reminds us of this in Acts 14:8-19, where he records what Paul and Barnabas went through at Lystra, modern day Turkey, a rather dangerous and inhospitable city for anyone, and especially those who proclaimed the Good News about the resurrected Jesus. While preaching at Lystra, Paul performed a miracle under the power of the Holy Spirit. Through this empowerment and his powerful preaching, he healed a man lame from birth. The pagan crowd went wild with adulation for Paul after this miraculous healing. Luke notes that no matter how hard Paul tried to convince the crowd that God was responsible for this miracle, the pagans simply would not believe him. They only wanted to worship and deify him and Barnabas.

Sadly, Paul was to learn rather quickly that people are often fickle and that fame is often fleeting, for only in a matter of minutes did the tide of adulation for Paul turn to disaster. This is how Luke describes what happened to

Paul after his Jewish enemies found out that he was in Lystra teaching about Christ. "Then some Jews came from Antioch and Iconium, and won the crowd over. They stoned Paul and dragged him outside the city, thinking he was dead" (Acts 14:19 NIV).

Can you imagine yourself being given deification status one moment and then being nearly stoned to death the next moment? (I believe Paul would have appreciated the message in the old country song sung by John Denver, "Some days are diamonds, some days are stone.")

Paul's experience at Lystra serves as an excellent example of the fleeting nature of fame. Unfortunately, this would not be the last time he experienced disaster and great harm. The Bible records that Paul fully understood the dangers he faced in spreading the Good News. For the Holy Spirit had warned him that everywhere he went to preach, hardships, and imprisonment would await him. But he did not care. He just went on preaching anyway. (Talk about courage and commitment.)

After reflecting on what Paul went through, the great question is how he was able to be content and keep on functioning. One way he was able to do this was by keeping the highs and lows of life in perspective. He knew that triumph and disaster often ride side by side in human nature. And he determined in his "Spirit" to keep life (triumph and disaster) in a balance. Let's listen to him explain how he did this:

> *"I have learned to be content whatever the circumstances. I know what it is to be in need, and I know what it is to have plenty. I have learned the secret of being content in any and every situation, whether well fed or hungry, whether living in*

CHAPTER 8: IF YOU CAN MEET WITH TRIUMPH AND DISASTER...

plenty or in want. I can do all this through him who gives me strength" (Philippians 4:11-13 NIV).

Paul's secret was that he learned, with God's help, to be content. (Have you learned to be content?) Does this sound too simple? Not if you have absolute faith in God, as Paul did. He just believed that God would strengthen him and encourage him when he faced great challenges and that all things would work out for the best. He understood that keeping life in perspective and never losing faith is the key to victory over whatever comes your way. Keep in mind that Paul wrote about the spiritual and emotional power of contentment while under house arrest, chained to a Roman guard.

In essence, Paul, who was a Rabbi, lawyer, and scholar (Acts 22:3), reminds us again and again, as did Kipling, that life will have its ups and downs, its triumphs and disasters.

But if we are in God's will, He will help us keep life in perspective and find the contentment and coping skills we will need when adversities come our way.

**"If you can meet with triumph and disaster
And treat those two impostors just the same:"**

THE SPIRITUAL WISDOM OF IF

"If you can meet with triumph and disaster
And treat those two impostors just the same:"

§§§

Meditate on These Related Wisdom-Filled Scriptures

"… Here on earth you will have many trials and sorrows; but cheer up, for I have overcome the world."
John 16:33 (LNT)

"Yet what we suffer now is nothing compared to the glory He will give us later."
Romans 8:18 (LNT)

"Rejoice always, pray constantly, give thanks in all circumstances …"
1 Thessalonians 5:16-18 (RSV)

"Therefore do not worry about tomorrow, for tomorrow will worry about itself. Each day has enough trouble of its own."
Matthew 6:34 (NIV)

How can you apply these Scriptures to your life?

CHAPTER 8: IF YOU CAN MEET WITH TRIUMPH AND DISASTER…

Remember, With God's Help:

§§§

- I will learn from my mistakes and failures.
- I will keep life in perspective, no matter what circumstances I find myself in.
- I will view my failures as a chance at a new beginning.

Remember to pray …
Dear God, as you did for Paul, help me keep my ups and downs in life in perspective and help me do what you would want me to do as I journey through life with all its trials and tribulations.

**"If you can meet with triumph and disaster
And treat those two impostors just the same:"**

What did you learn from this chapter?

Chapter 9
"If you can bear to hear the truth you've spoken Twisted by knaves to make a trap for fools,"

Jesus could. Can you?
Book of Matthew, Chapter 4
Book of Luke, Chapter 4: 1-13

Jesus knew only too well about half-truths and innuendos, and He reminds us that they are sometimes more damaging to a person than an outright lie and just as painful to bear. If one takes a hard look at Jesus' life, one would be hard pressed not to wonder how He withstood all the lies, distortions, and twisted words that were spoken against Him throughout His ministry. But as we know He did withstand these vicious dishonest verbal attacks. As Kipling would say, Jesus could bear to hear the truth He spoke twisted by knaves. (With God's help so can you.)

> knave:
> a tricky, deceitful fellow.
>
> Webster's New World
> Dictionary, 2nd Ed.

Luke gives us an excellent example of how Satan used "twisted" words and incorrect Scriptures to tempt and mislead Jesus.

Let me set the scene for this example by noting that Jesus was led into the wilderness for 40 days where He fasted and prayed. And because of his fasting, he became very hungry and weak. (Remember, Satan will try to attack you when you feel weak and helpless. He will go

CHAPTER 9: IF YOU CAN BEAR TO HEAR THE TRUTH...

after your most vulnerable spot. Be prepared.)

Luke wrote that Satan tried three times to get Jesus to "switch sides" and worship him. But, because of Jesus' Scriptural knowledge, he was able to use a quote from the Hebrew Bible to refute each of Satan's attempts to mislead and trick him.

In essence, Jesus just would not give in to Satan's trickery. And because He would not give in, Satan temporarily gave up. (Remember, Satan never gives up.)

Jesus reminds us that one way to overcome those who try to trick you with dishonest Scriptural knowledge is to know the Word and obey it. "And you shall know the truth, and the truth shall make you free" (John 8:32 KJV).

> Ask God to help you know the difference between a correct use of Scripture and an incorrect one.

In Mark 14:55-59, we find another example of blatant dishonesty that Jesus had to endure when the Sanhedrin, the Jewish ruling body, became so upset with Him that they plotted to get rid of Him by any means possible. Because of their hatred of Jesus, they forced Him to endure six illegal trials. The authorities who tried Him did not care about pursuing the truth, they just wanted Jesus out of their hair. They wanted Him dead. Since they could not find anything to accuse Him of, they just made up lies and twisted the truth He spoke. Mark noted their dishonesty and hatred for Jesus with this comment, "The chief priests and the whole Sanhedrin were looking for evidence against Jesus so they could put Him to death, but they did not find any. Many testified falsely" (Mark 14:55-57 NIV). Sadly, not one person or friend testified for Jesus during these rigged trials. (Where are your friends when you need them?)

Although these examples of verbal dishonesty against Jesus relate to spiritual matters, they have practical applications for us today. For instance, Kipling's couplet and the Scriptures I emphasized in this chapter should remind us to be vigilant, cautious, and discerning when dealing with deceitful and dubious people.

> Remember:
> The Bible can be a used for good or evil depending upon the motives of those interpreting it.

Paul also knew something about deceitful people. He reminds us in Philippians 1:10 to pray for wisdom and discernment (as did Solomon) on how to deal with people who may want to harm, mislead, or trick us. The writer of Hebrews also challenges us to train our minds "to distinguish good from evil" (Hebrews 5:14 NIV).

> Be aware of character assassins.

In sum, we need to remember that there will always be those (knaves) who want to twist the truth we have spoken and who want to manipulate and harm us for their own selfish reasons. But, if we **seek God's wisdom** and **develop a spiritual and moral compass**, He will speak to our hearts and help direct us on how to respond to those mean and dishonest people who we will encounter on our journey through life.

**"If you can bear to hear the truth you've spoken
Twisted by knaves to make a trap for fools,"**

CHAPTER 9: IF YOU CAN BEAR TO HEAR THE TRUTH...

"If you can bear to hear the truth you've spoken
Twisted by knaves to make a trap for fools,"

§§§

Meditate on These Related Wisdom-Filled Scriptures

"If anyone can control his tongue, it proves that he has perfect control over his self in every other way … So also the tongue is a small thing, but what enormous damage it can do."
James 3:2 and 5 (TLB)

"Beware of false prophets, which come to you in sheep's clothing, but inwardly they are ravening wolves."
Matthew 7:15 (KJV)

"Reckless words pierce like a sword, but the tongue of the wise brings healing."
Proverbs 12:18 (NIV)

"Anyone who says he is a Christian but doesn't control his sharp tongue is just fooling himself, and his religion isn't worth much."
James 1:26 (TLB)

How can you apply these Scriptures to your life?

Remember, With God's Help:

§§§

- I will remember that the spoken word is often sharper than a two-edged sword.
- I will not allow dishonest people to tear me down.

Remember to pray …
Dear God, pick me up and comfort me when others try to hurt me through their dishonest comments and innuendos.

**"If you can bear to hear the truth you've spoken
Twisted by knaves to make a trap for fools,"**

What did you learn from this chapter?

Chapter 10
"Or watch the things you gave your life to, broken, And stoop and build'em up with worn-out tools;"

Job did. Can you?
Book of Job

The book of Job reminds us that life is often difficult, unfair, and hard to fathom or understand. The story of Job reminds us that there are just some things we will never comprehend about life or about God.

> "O the depth of the riches both of the wisdom and knowledge of God! how unsearchable are his judgments, and his ways past finding out!"
> Romans 11:33 (KJV)

The Bible notes that Job was a prosperous man who truly loved God with all of his heart. He was also blessed with a beautiful family, good health, and was well respected in his community. The Bible goes on to record that Satan took a special interest in Job. He told God that the only reason Job was faithful and loved Him was because of all the blessings God had bestowed upon him. Satan made a bet with God that if these blessings were taken away, Job would curse God and lose his faith. For reasons that are hard to comprehend, God allowed Satan to test Job. The only thing God would not allow

> "It is not suffering as such that troubles us. It is undeserved suffering."
> Eugene H. Peterson, "Introduction to Job" (MSG)

Satan to do was to kill him. (Do you sometimes feel that God allows Satan to test you? I do.)

As we know from Scripture, Satan really went after Job. He took all his blessings away one by one. In essence, Job literally watched the things he gave his life to disappear – health, children, money, friends. Conditions became so bad for Job that his own wife begged him to curse God and die. (How would you like to be married to her?) But Job would not give up on God.

And, to make matters worse, his three so-called friends, Eliphaz, Bildad, and Zophar, thought Job's problems were the result of some sin he had committed and they begged him to confess and ask God for forgiveness. Of course, we know from Scripture that Job had not done anything to bring on the Satanic attacks. The Bible goes on to record that Elihu, another fair-weather friend, also sermonized for Job to repent of something so that God would restore him to his former status in life.

> When the Civil War was at its worst, Lincoln was caught by Mary Lincoln's dressmaker, Elizabeth Keckley, reading the book of Job.
> "The Atlantic," October 2005

Sadly, Job reminds us that sometimes our friends and loved ones may not understand what we are going through. For Job knew in his heart that he had not done anything wrong and could not understand why he was being punished, and not knowing why caused him great pain and anguish. He even cried out that he wished that he had never been born. But he hung in there, trusted God, and never wavered from his faith and belief.

Job reminds us that even though we may not fully

> Sometimes we don't know why we suffer, but we must be willing to trust that God, in His mysterious ways, knows the overall plan for our lives.

CHAPTER 10: WATCH THE THINGS YOU GAVE YOUR LIFE TO, BROKEN

understand the "whys" of suffering, we must not give up hope. (We must believe that in the end things will work out for the best.) Remember what Joseph said to his brothers in Genesis 5:20, "You intended to harm me, but God intended it for good ..." (NIV) (Do you trust God enough to wait patiently for Him to bring something good out of your bad situations?)

> "Suffering is a mystery, and Job comes to respect the mystery."
> Eugene H. Peterson,
> "Introduction to Job" (MSG)

In the end, God honored Job's faith, and the Bible records that God restored him and blessed him tenfold with children, possessions, land, and wealth. Job's example reminds us that as believers we need to stay focused on what is right in God's eyes, no matter what the enemy throws our way. Through all his trials and tribulations, Job never sinned, cursed, or blamed God for his problems. He once shouted, "Though he slay me, yet will I trust in him" (Job 13:15 KJV). What great faith! (God help us to have this type of faith!)

Although I am not advocating suffering, we know that on a human level suffering and your response to it can help strengthen your testimony. That is one reason why Alcoholics Anonymous is so effective. It is a program in which a person with an addiction that he or she has under control helps another person struggling with a similar addiction. People can connect and relate with someone who has

> I walked a mile with Pleasure;
> She chatted all the way;
> But left me none the wiser
> For all she had to say.
>
> I walked a mile with Sorrow,
> And ne'er a word said she;
> But, oh! The things I learned from her,
> When sorrow walked with me.
> Robert Browning (1812-1889)

felt the same pain or gone through the same struggles as they have. It makes the person relatable and gives them credibility. The writer of Hebrews reminds us that Jesus was able to relate to those who suffered and were tempted, "Because he himself suffered when he was tempted, he is able to help those who are being tempted" (Hebrews 2:18 NIV).

> "I don't trust a man who hasn't suffered ..."
>
> John Eldredge
> "Wild at Heart"

In sum, let me quote from a footnote in the NIV *Life Application Study Bible*,

> *"Remember Job's greatest test was not the pain, but that he did not know why he was suffering. Our greatest test may be that we must trust God's goodness even though we don't understand why our lives are going in a certain way. We must learn to trust in God who is good and not in the goodness of life." (Job 33:13)*

Can you do this?

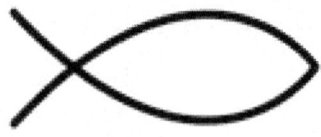

**"Or watch the things you gave your life to, broken,
And stoop and build 'em up with worn-out tools;"**

CHAPTER 10: WATCH THE THINGS YOU GAVE YOUR LIFE TO, BROKEN

"Or watch the things you gave your life to, broken,
And stoop and build'em up with worn-out tools;"

§§§

Meditate on These Related Wisdom-Filled Scriptures

"He healeth the broken in heart, and bindeth up their wounds."
Psalm 147:3 (KJV)

"The Lord upholdeth all that fall, and raiseth up all those that be bowed down."
Psalm 145:14 (KJV)

"As you know, we consider blessed those who have persevered. You have heard of Job's perseverance and have seen what the Lord finally brought about."
James 5:10-11 (KJV)

"When you pass through the waters,
I will be with you.
And when you pass through the rivers,
they will not sweep over you.
When you walk through the fire,
you will not be burned;
the flames will not set you ablaze.
Since you are precious and honored in my sight
and because I love you ...
Do not be afraid, for I am with you."
Isaiah 43:2, 4, 5 (NIV)

"And we know that in all things God works for the good of those who love Him, who have been called according to His purpose."
Romans 8:28 (NIV)

How can you apply these Scriptures to your life?

CHAPTER 10: WATCH THE THINGS YOU GAVE YOUR LIFE TO, BROKEN

Remember, With God's Help:

§§§

- I will use hard times to strengthen me, to pick myself up, and start anew.
- I will be able to handle the tragedies and crises that come my way in life.
- I will not become bitter when things seem to be trying to break me down.

Remember to pray …
Dear God, as you did for Job, give me the strength to face and overcome whatever adversities come my way.

**"Or watch the things you gave your life to, broken,
And stoop and build'em up with worn-out tools;"**

What did you learn from this chapter?

With God's help I will work on acquiring and developing these personality traits.

Stanza Three

If you can make one heap of all your winnings
And risk it on one turn of pitch-and-toss,
And lose, and start again at your beginnings,
And never breathe a word about your loss:
If you can force your heart and nerve and sinew
To serve your turn long after they are gone,
And so hold on when there is nothing in you
Except the Will which says to them: "Hold on!"

Have you memorized this character-building stanza?

Chapter 11
"If you can make one heap of all your winnings
And risk it on one turn of pitch-and-toss,
And lose, and start again at your beginnings,
And never breathe a word about your loss;"

The disciples did. Can you?
Matthew 19:27-29
The Investment Parable
Matthew 25:14-30

> **Parable:**
> a short story that illustrates a spiritual principle or moral attitude

Although Kipling was probably talking about financial risk-taking when he penned these lines to his son, I believe these lines would have been relevant to the 12 original disciples who risked it all to follow Jesus. For example, Peter said to Jesus, "We left everything to follow You. What will we get out of it" (Matthew 19:27 TLB)? Good question.

Now ask yourself what you would do if Jesus came into your house and said to you, "Don't worry about your family, your house, your friends, or your money. Don't think, just do what I am asking you to do. Trust and follow me." (Could you do this?) We know that Peter and the other disciples were so profoundly moved by the awesomeness of Jesus that they immediately left everything behind to follow Him. And what was their reward for this monumental and spontaneous decision?

Jesus promises that those who follow Him "shall

receive a hundred times as much in return, and shall have eternal life (Matthew 19:29 NIV). Why would Jesus ask them to drop everything and follow Him? Because He is reminding them that He wants them to get their priorities straight and stay focused on Him and His purpose for their life, not mundane things or material possessions. Now, what was Jesus's purpose for their lives?

In essence, His purpose and charge to this motley crew was for them to travel the highways and byways of the world and spread the gospel to others and make believers of them. Which was not an easy task for the original 12 disciples. For the Bible records that many of the people the disciples tried to convert became angry because they did not want to change or be converted.

Thus, the disciples were often in grave danger and harm. And because of the dangers they faced, some Biblical scholars suggest that 11 of the 12 disciples met with violent deaths. But they were not afraid because they were empowered by the Holy Spirit and nothing would keep them from doing what God had called them to do. (Acts 1:8)

Remember, none of the original 12 disciples were learned scholars, religious experts, or saints. They were just ordinary humans given an extraordinary challenge, and that was to follow Christ and spread the Gospel. And because they were human and fallible, I'm sure that they were ecstatic on the days when they won souls over for the Lord and then temporarily dejected on other days when they were hounded and chased out of town.

But as the Bible reminds us, they did not dwell long upon their circumstances or feelings. As Kipling would say, they didn't breathe a word about their feelings or loss. After a bad experience they just geared up, moved

CHAPTER 11: IF YOU CAN MAKE ONE HEAP...

on, and started preaching again. They were fired up and passionate about their mission. Risk-taking did not bother them. And it should not bother us if we are doing what God directs us to do.

The Investment Story

Another example of risk-taking is found in Matthew 25:14-30 where the emphasis is on using whatever talents, abilities, or gifts God has given us to serve Him

> Are you using your talents/gifts to honor and serve God? If so, how?

and further the kingdom. For example, God uses the investment parable to illuminate His desire for us to be wise stewards of money.

In brief, the investment parable is about a successful financial master who was preparing to go on an extended trip, but before he left, he called in three of his servants and He gave each of them a sum of money to invest wisely. (In this parable money is called a talent. One talent today would be approximately $300,000.)

To one of his servants, he gave five talents, ($1,500,000). To the second servant, he gave two ($600,000). To the third, he gave one ($300,000). Then he left. The first two made money for their master, but the third servant was scared to take a risk because of the fear of losing his masters money. So, he decided to dig a hole and bury it. The master became furious with him because he did not make him any money. In anger, the master probably said something like, "You could have at least put my money in a CD where it would have drawn some interest." Notice the third servant did not do anything wrong. He did not squander or lose the money. He just hid it. As my son-in-law's former pastor Ralph Mann noted, "Some of us do that with our lives: we don't do anything wrong, we just don't do anything."

In sum, Jesus reminds us in this parable that He wants us to take risks especially if they honor the virtues and values that are discussed throughout the Bible. He wants us to witness for Him and care for others. He wants us to serve Him wisely with our gifts, talents, abilities, and our time. And He wants us to do it with passion and enthusiasm.

God also reminds us that if we are in a rut, we should do something about it. Remember, God wants us to seek His will, not our will, and then make the changes we need to make to fulfill His purpose for our life. As Moses noted in Deuteronomy 1:6-8, "You have stayed here long enough on this mountain: move on…" (MSG)

(Do you need to move on or to make some changes in your life? Then, do it! Don't live with despair or regrets.)

Never forget, life is short. Time is precious.
God does not want us to waste it or squander it.

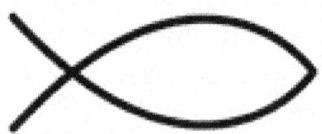

"If you can make one heap of all your winnings
And risk it on one turn of pitch-and-toss,
And lose, and start again at your beginnings,
And never breathe a word about your loss;"

CHAPTER 11: IF YOU CAN MAKE ONE HEAP...

"If you can make one heap of all your winnings
And risk it on one turn of pitch-and-toss,
And lose, and start again at your beginnings,
And never breathe a word about your loss;"

§§§

Meditate on These Related Wisdom-Filled Scriptures

"He who trusts in the Lord will prosper."
Proverbs 28:25 (NIV)

"We toss the coin, but it is the Lord who controls its decision."
Proverbs 16:33 (TLB)

"A good person survives misfortune, but a wicked life invites disaster."
Proverbs 12:26 (MSG)

"If anyone would come after me, he must deny himself and take up his cross and follow me."
Matthew 16:24 (NIV)

How can you apply these Scriptures to your life?

Remember, With God's Help:

§§§

- I can take risks.
- I can influence my environment and not just react to it.
- I will not wallow in self-pity when I fail, but will pick myself up and start again.

Remember to pray …
Dear God, stir me to seek your wisdom if I need to take a risk or make a change in my life and, if so, give me the courage to do it.

**"If you can make one heap of all your winnings
And risk it on one turn of pitch-and-toss,
And lose, and start again at your beginnings,
And never breathe a word about your loss;"**

What did you learn from this chapter?

Chapter 12
"If you can force your heart and nerve and sinew to serve your turn long after they are gone, and so hold on when there is nothing in you except the Will which says to them: 'Hold on!'"

Paul held on. Can you hold on?
Book of 2 Corinthians

Paul was divinely inspired and blessed by God. He was highly educated, articulate, motivated, and a great encourager. He was a man on a mission. His obsession and calling was to spread the Good News about Christ throughout the world. But, he paid a big price for this commitment. Take a minute and reflect on what Paul had to endure for his commitment to spread the Good News, and then ask yourself if you would be willing to pay the price Paul did to do something that God laid on your heart. Paul wrote this about his trials and tribulations:

> *"Five times I received from the Jews thirty-nine lashes. Three times I was beaten with rods, once I was stoned, three times shipwrecked... I have been on frequent journeys, in dangers from rivers, in dangers from robbers, dangers from countrymen, dangers from the Gentiles, dangers in the city, dangers in the wilderness, dangers on the sea, dangers from false brethren; I have been in labor*

*and hardship, through many sleepless nights, in hunger and thirst, often without food, in cold and exposure. Apart from such external things, there is the daily pressure upon me of concern for all the churches" (*2 Corinthians 11:24-28 NASB).

To add to the above challenges, Paul also suffered from a handicap. He called it his "thorn in my flesh" (2 Corinthians 12:7, NIV). We don't know what it was, but whatever it was, he did not want it. Three times he asked God to remove this malady. God said no all three times. God told Paul, "My grace is sufficient for you, for my power is made perfect in weakness" (2 Corinthians 12:9, NIV). I doubt that this was the answer that Paul wanted to hear, but he did not question God's decision. This condition kept him humble and in contact with God. He accepted God's decision and moved on with his mission in life.

Paul reminds us just how hard it is for a person to hold on and function when they are emotionally, physically, financially, and spiritually exhausted and depleted. The question is how Paul was able to hold on,

> In 1962, Martin Luther King, Jr. wrote his famous Civil Rights letter while in a Birmingham, Alabama jail.

function, and witness. For example, where did he get the strength to write Philippians while in prison? The answer is that Paul knew and believed in his heart that God is ultimately in charge. And that everything will work out for those who don't give up and who keep their eyes focused on Him and His word.

The Bible notes in Philippians 4:11-13 that Paul never took his eye off the mark or wavered in his ultimate purpose, which was to spread the Good News.

CHAPTER 12: IF YOU CAN FORCE YOUR HEART...

As I have previously mentioned, no matter what circumstances Paul found himself in, he **learned** to cope and be content. He just willed

> "Then Jesus told his disciples a parable to show them that they should always pray and not give up."
> Luke 18:1 (NIV)

himself mentally, physically, and spiritually to hold on and keep on. When I feel sorry for myself, I often think about what Paul went through, and then I pray to God to give me a little of what he had.

As I pen these words, I have just had my prostate removed. Believe me, this is not something I wanted to do. Paul reminds me, though, not to let this condition and its unintended consequences keep me from striving to become a Spiritual Hall of Famer and the man God wants me to be. Paul reminds us that if we are about the Lord's business and in His will, He will give us the strength to hold on when we feel like we can't hold on.

In closing, I want you to pause and reflect on what Paul said when his time on earth was about up. He said, "I have fought the good fight, I have finished the race, I have kept the faith; …" (2 Timothy 4:7 RSV).

The question is:
Can you fight the good fight? Can you finish the race?
Can you keep the faith?

**"If you can force your heart and nerve and sinew
To serve your turn long after they are gone,
And so hold on when there is nothing in you
Except the Will which says to them: 'Hold on!'"**

"If you can force your heart and nerve and sinew
To serve your turn long after they are gone,
And so hold on when there is nothing in you
Except the Will which says to them: 'Hold on!'"

§§§

Meditate on These Related Wisdom-Filled Scriptures

"When I pray, you answer me, and encourage me by giving me the strength I need."
Psalms 138:3 (TLB)

"If you hold on to me for dear life," says God,
"I'll get you out of any trouble.
I'll give you the best of care,
If you'll only get to know and trust me.
Call me and I'll answer ..."
Psalms 91:14-16 (MSG)

"I can do all things through Christ which strengtheneth me."
Philippians 4:13 (KJV)

How can you apply these Scriptures to your life?

CHAPTER 12: IF YOU CAN FORCE YOUR HEART...

Remember, With God's Help:

§§§

- I will pick myself up and keep going when I am faced with mental, spiritual, and physical challenges.
- I will never give in to adversity.
- I will force myself to keep going until my time on this earth is up.

Remember to pray …
Dear God, as you did for Paul, give me the strength to hold on and function when I begin to feel that I cannot hold on.

**"If you can force your heart and nerve and sinew
To serve your turn long after they are gone,
And so hold on when there is nothing in you
Except the Will which says to them: 'Hold on!'"**

What did you learn from this chapter?

With God's help I will work on acquiring and developing these personality traits.

Stanza Four

If you can talk with crowds and keep your virtue,
Or walk with Kings – nor lose the common touch,
If neither foes nor loving friends can hurt you,
If all men count with you, but none too much:
If you can fill the unforgiving minute
With sixty seconds' worth of distance run,
Yours is the Earth and everything that's in it,
And – which is more – you'll be a Man, my son!

Have you memorized this character-building stanza?

Chapter 13
"If you can talk with crowds and keep your virtue,
Or walk with Kings—nor lose the common touch,"

Esther could. Can you?
Book of Esther

Esther, queen of Persia, personifies the behavior described in this couplet. Because of her courage and persona, she is one of the most talked-about heroines in the Bible. As Kipling would say, she did not lose her virtue or the common touch. She displayed courage, compassion, modesty, sincerity, tactfulness, and humility. This wise, inspired queen understood that "When pride comes, then comes disgrace, but with humility comes wisdom" (Proverbs 11:2 NIV).

> "Do not be proud, but be willing to associate with people of low position. Do not be conceited."
> Romans 12:16 (NIV)

The Bible notes that Esther did not start out with a silver spoon. She was an orphan who was fortunate enough to be raised by a loving, wise, caring, and Godly cousin named Mordecai. He was a powerful, positive influence in her life. (Those who do not have Godly, loving, and caring parents need to pray for wise role models like Mordecai to help them navigate through life.)

Due to her beauty and character and through fortuitous circumstances, Esther became the queen of the most powerful nation in the world. But this young queen was soon to face a dilemma that is hard for most of us to fathom. She was spiritually challenged to try to save her fellow Jews and her cousin Mordecai from extermination and from Haman, the king's top official.

Scripture notes that Haman was an evil, mean-spirited, attention-seeking individual who basically wanted everyone to defer to him. Something Mordecai refused to do. And, because Mordecai would not defer to him, Haman hated him. Mordecai reminded Haman that he gave allegiance only to God.

One day, after Mordecai again refused to bow to him, Haman concocted a plot to kill him. And because of his hatred of the Jews, he also devised a plan to destroy them. (Haman was the Adolf Hitler of his day.) Haman's devious plan was initially approved by the king. Fortunately, Mordecai found out about the edict to kill all the Jews and asked Esther to intervene with the king. He challenged her with these often-quoted and passionate words:

> *"Don't think that just because you live in the king's house you're the one Jew who will get out of this alive. If you persist in staying silent in a time like this, help and deliverance will arrive for the Jews from someplace else; but you and your family will be wiped out. **Who knows? Maybe you were made queen for just such a time as this**"* (Esther 4:13-14 MSG, emphasis mine).

In essence, Mordecai reminded Esther how blessed she was. And He challenged her to stand up, be brave, and do what God wanted her to do, which was to save her people.

CHAPTER 13: IF YOU CAN TALK WITH CROWDS...

As Esther grappled with her uncle's challenge, she realized she was treading on dangerous ground because, as was the custom of the time, one was not to approach the king without being invited. To do so was to face instant death. But after much prayer and fasting, Esther decided to take a risk, and develop a plan of action to approach the king. Think about the courage it took to do this. And while Esther was developing a plan to get the king to counteract the edict to exterminate her people, God miraculously intervened to help her. For God nudged the king to read some historical documents that noted Mordecai was a good man who had once saved his life. After this God-inspired revelation, the king decided to honor and reward Mordecai for his loyalty. (Due to some twisted thinking, Haman thought he was the one to be honored.)

> **Jesus said:**
>
> "From everyone who has been given much, much will be demanded; and from the one who has been entrusted with much, much more will be asked."
>
> Luke 12:48 (NIV)

> **Talk About Courage**
>
> "And thus I will go in to the king, which is not according to the law; and if I perish, I perish."
>
> Esther 4:16 (NASB)

After some soul searching, Esther decided to tell the king at a dinner she had planned for him that if Haman's plan to kill all the Jews succeeded, she and Mordecai would die because they were also Jews. Because of the king's feelings for Esther and Mordecai, this revelation so upset and angered him that he momentarily stormed out of the room. While he was gone, Haman threw himself on the queen's couch and pleaded for mercy.

When the king walked back in, he assumed Haman was molesting the queen, and this really set him off. And, when the upset king was told that Haman had erected a gallows next to his house where he was planning on hanging Mordecai, the angry king ordered that Haman be hanged on it instead. Ironically, Haman ended up losing his own life because of his vanity and outright vindictiveness. (You reap what you sow.)

As I have noted, Esther was an unusual and caring queen who never lost the common touch nor forgot about those she ruled over. Remember, Esther could have kept her mouth shut and played it safe about her Jewish identity and continued on with her privileged life.

> Do you speak out when you see evil or do you play it safe and remain silent?

In essence, this courageous lady reminds us to seek God's will when we are faced with challenges and adversities. She also reminds us that no matter what high status we achieve in life, excessive ego and pride are not virtues that we should flaunt or be proud of. Esther also challenges us to be compassionate toward those less fortunate than we are.

Finally, Esther reminds us that one person can make a big difference in society and in people's lives.

What kind of difference are you making?

**"If you can talk with crowds and keep your virtue,
Or walk with Kings – nor lose the common touch,"**

CHAPTER 13: IF YOU CAN TALK WITH CROWDS...

"If you can talk with crowds and keep your virtue,
Or walk with Kings – nor lose the common touch,"

§§§

Meditate on These Related Wisdom-Filled Scriptures

"He who gains by oppressing the poor or by bribing the rich, shall end in poverty."
Proverbs 25:15 (TLB)

"Pride disgusts the Lord. Take my word for it – proud men shall be punished."
Proverbs 16:16 (TLB)

"If a man comes into your church dressed in expensive clothes and with valuable gold rings on his fingers, and at the same moment another man comes in who is poor and dressed in threadbare clothes, and you make a lot of fuss over the rich man and give him the best seat in the house and say to the poor man, 'You can stand over there if you like, or else sit on the floor' – well, judging a man by his wealth shows that you are guided by wrong motives."
James 2:2 (TLB)

"… For a man's heart determines his speech."
Matthew 12:34 (NLT)

"A good man's speech reveals the rich treasures within him. An evil-hearted man is filled with venom, and his speech reveals it.
Matthew 12:35 (NLT)

"Do not be proud, but be willing to associate with people of low position. Do not be conceited."
Romans 12:16 (NIV)

"From everyone who has been given much, much will be demanded; and from the one who has been entrusted with much, much more will be asked."
Luke 12:48 (NIV)

How can you apply these Scriptures to your life?

CHAPTER 13: IF YOU CAN TALK WITH CROWDS...

Remember, With God's Help:

§§§

- I will be honest when I talk to crowds or individuals.
- I will remember that the Lord does not want me to lose the common touch.
- I will not let myself be ruled by pride.

Remember to pray …
Dear God, remind me to be sensitive and considerate to others, no matter what their status in life. And give me that Esther-like courage and desire to stand up for those who are mistreated and have no power.

**"If you can talk with crowds and keep your virtue,
Or walk with Kings – nor lose the common touch,"**

What did you learn from this chapter?

Chapter 14
"If neither foes nor loving friends can hurt you
If all men count with you, but none too much:"

Jesus understood this.
And so did Paul. Do you?
Books of Matthew, Luke, and 2 Timothy

We know that nothing is more painful or harmful than being betrayed or humiliated by a spouse or a person that we consider to be a close friend or loved one. We probably shouldn't be surprised when our foes try to hurt us, but friends, or so-called friends, are another matter.

Jesus understood this type of pain. Because he was betrayed by two of his disciples, Peter and Judas. Even though it was preordained, what anguish He must have felt.

> Remember:
> Changing circumstances may cause relationships to change dramatically.

The Bible records that Peter was one of Jesus' favorite disciples. He even healed Peter's mother-in-law. Peter loved Jesus deeply and said that there was no way he would ever betray him or deny him. But when his life was threatened by Jesus' enemies, he lied. For the Scriptures note that he did deny Jesus, not once but three times. (Matthew 26:35) At his last act of denial, Peter was so distraught because of his cowardice and shame that he begged Jesus to forgive him. (Of course, Jesus did.) Thus Peter was given a second chance to become a mighty warrior for God. (Remember, God is in the second chance

CHAPTER 14: IF NEITHER FOES NOR LOVING FRIENDS...

and forgiveness business. Aren't we glad?)

For whatever reasons, Judas Iscariot's betrayal took a different turn and twist. The book of Matthew implies that greed was the reason for Judas turning Jesus over to those who hated Him and wanted Him killed. But we also find in Luke 22:3 and John 13:2 that Judas allowed Satan to enter into his mind and influence him, which some scholars believe led him to betray Jesus. The Bible notes that after Judas turned Jesus over to his enemies, Judas became so depressed that he hanged himself. Unlike Peter, he did not ask for forgiveness and could not overcome his betrayal.

Another example of betrayal is highlighted in Colossians 4:14, which describes Paul being deserted and forsaken by Demas, who he thought was a good friend. This betrayal deeply hurt Paul because of what they had been through together. (2 Timothy 4:9-10)

Sadly, we are also reminded that even the great apostle Paul had trouble with relationships. Luke writes in Acts 15:36 that Paul had an angry confrontation with his best friend Barnabas, a man who helped launch Paul's ministry. This caused them to quit traveling together. (They later made up.)

Scripture and Kipling remind us that we must be on guard against placing too much emphasis or significance on another person. Because if we are emotionally wounded by a significant other, or if a friend turns out not to be who he or she claims to be, the results to our health and outlook can be devastating.

The Bible records that God wants us to love and care deeply about people. He just wants us to remember that there are no absolute guarantees (as does Kipling) when it comes to predicting and understanding human behavior. Thus God uses Paul to remind us that when we really want to get to know someone or have a meaningful relationship, we need to look below the surface at that person and not just be visually or emotionally stimulated. Paul wants us to look at their heart, their character, and their actions. God reminds us to be discerning and careful about who we place our trust in. As Solomon noted in Proverbs 22:3, "A prudent person foresees danger and takes precautions. The simpleton goes blindly on and suffers the consequences." (NIV)

> "Test all things ..."
> 1 Thessalonians 5:21
> (NKJV)

Of course, the big question is, who do you call upon when your best friend, your spouse, your lover, or your kids betray you? The answer should be God or someone God directs you to. Remember, if you need someone so badly that you feel you cannot live without them, you may be heading for trouble. God is the only one you should feel you cannot live without. God promises, "I will never fail you. I will never abandon you" (Hebrews 13:5 NLT).

§§§

I also believe there is another teachable interpretation in this couplet under discussion. For instance, when people do count with you don't forget to thank them for what they did for you.

When I read and reflect upon this couplet, I often think of Jesus' insightful parable found in Luke 17:11-19. When you are pained by the lack of gratitude for something you have done for someone, I suggest you read this parable. In the main, this parable tells of Jesus healing 10 lepers, but unbelievably only one of the 10 he healed came back to thank him. And I believe Jesus was pained and hurt for a brief moment by the ingratitude of the nine who did not acknowledge his help, because he asked in verse 17, "Didn't I

CHAPTER 14: IF NEITHER FOES NOR LOVING FRIENDS...

heal ten men? Where are the nine? ..." (TLB) To me, Jesus is reminding us how important it is to acknowledge and show appreciation when it is warranted.

Many years later, William James, considered by some the father of American psychology, echoed one of the themes I believe Jesus was trying to convey in this parable when he noted, "The deepest principle in human nature is the craving to be appreciated."

Mr. Rogers, the late, great children's television host, also understood the importance of acknowledging those who have cared for us and helped us become who we are. For example, Mr. Rogers adopted the habit of asking his audience when he gave public speeches to pause for a moment of silence and think about those who made a difference in their lives.

> Have you thought about and thanked those who have made a difference in your life?

In sum, God does not want us to be naive when dealing with people, nor did Kipling. God also wants us to stop and think before we enter into a relationship or get into a situation that we are not sure of. The Scriptures remind us to pray for wisdom and discernment when we have to make tough decisions. God also wants us to develop the attitude of gratitude.

"If neither foes nor loving friends can hurt you
If all men count with you, but none too much:"

"If neither foes nor loving friends can hurt you
If all men count with you, but none too much:"

§§§

Meditate on These Related Wisdom-Filled Scriptures

"There are 'friends' who pretend to be friends, but there is a friend who sticks closer than a brother."
Proverbs 18:24 (TLB)

"Only a simpleton believes what he is told! A prudent man checks to see where he is going."
Proverbs 14:15 (TLB)

"A wise man is cautious and avoids danger; a fool plunges ahead with great confidence."
Proverbs 14:16 (TLB)

"Paul thanked the Philippians for helping him in his ministry."
Philippians 4:9 (MSG)

How can you apply these Scriptures to your life?

CHAPTER 14: IF NEITHER FOES NOR LOVING FRIENDS...

Remember, With God's Help:

§§§

- I will pray for discernment when I am facing adversity or having to make a tough decision.
- I will remember that, no matter what happens to me or who hurts me, God is always there for me.
- I will thank those who helped me or cared for me.

Remember to pray …
Dear God, thank you for being there when others let me down or hurt me. And remind me to pray for wisdom and discernment when I'm faced with relationship decisions.

**"If neither foes nor loving friends can hurt you
If all men count with you, but none too much:"**

What did you learn from this chapter?

Chapter 15
"If you can fill the unforgiving minute
With sixty seconds' worth of distance run,"

Ruth and Naomi could. Can you?
Book of Ruth

What do you do when you receive the bad news (you name it), what Kipling called the unforgiving minute?

For example, how would you react to this scenario: you have just lost your husband at a young age, you have no insurance, no children to help you out, no rich friends who will take you in, no Social Security, plus you have a recently widowed mother-in-law who cannot take care of herself financially. Well, this is the predicament that Ruth found herself in.

The writer of Ruth in the Old Testament gives us a vivid account of how Ruth coped with the shocking loss of her husband and her dire circumstances. And the writer noted that one way she did this was by making a life commitment to take care of her widowed mother-in-law, Naomi. She also chose to worship Naomi's God.

To add to Ruth's painful set of circumstances, the Bible notes that Orpah, Ruth's sister-in-law, also lost her husband at about the same time as Ruth did. Now the plot thickens. You have three widows who are grieving and in deep financial straits and are searching for ways to cope and survive.

Remember, at the time Ruth lived, women had

CHAPTER 15: IF YOU CAN FILL THE UNFORGIVING MINUTE...

few, if any, rights that mattered. Thankfully, Naomi, who was a wise and a caring mother-in-law, had a plan of action. For starters, she knew that Ruth and Orpah had a better chance at a new and better life if they went back to their mothers. Because they were still relatively young and pretty, Naomi knew their chances of remarrying were great. But neither one of them wanted to abandon her. Naomi finally talked Orpah into going back to her home. But Ruth would not under any circumstances abandon her mother-in-law. After much thought and prayer, Naomi decided it would be best for her and Ruth to return to her hometown.

> **Loyalty and Commitment**
>
> "But, Ruth replied, 'Don't urge me to leave you or to turn back from you. Where you go I will go, and where you stay I will stay. Your people will be my people and your God my God. Where you die I will die, and there I will be buried. May the Lord deal with me, be it ever so severely, if anything but death separated you and me.'"
>
> Ruth 1:16 (NIV)

As we know from Scripture, Ruth did not wallow in her self-pity an unreasonable amount of time. When she got to Naomi's hometown, she just did whatever she had to do to survive. Because of the custom of the time, the poor were allowed to pick up any crops that were left in the field at harvest. As you might guess, Ruth went out and gathered what crops she could so she and Naomi had something to eat. Take a minute and reflect on how hard this work must have been for Ruth – all the bending, picking, and walking in all kinds of weather.

But Ruth never complained, she just did what she had to do. Ruth reminds us that sometimes we have to do what is right, even if it is not comfortable, convenient, or satisfying.

The Bible goes on to record that a man named

Boaz, who happened to be kin to Naomi, was quite impressed with Ruth's compassion and commitment to her mother-in-law.

To fast forward, this story has a happy ending. For Naomi recognized that Boaz was a little smitten with Ruth and suggested how she might approach Boaz about marriage. Her suggestions worked, because they do fall in love, get married, and have a child.

> Pray for a Naomi – a parent, a friend, a relative, or encourager who looks out for you and your best interests.

Although the story of Ruth is basically about Ruth's love for and commitment to Naomi, it is also a beautiful story about how two people overcame terrible losses and learned to help and encourage each other.

Ruth's and Naomi's predicament, like the story of Job, reminds us that life is often unfair, cruel, and unpredictable. And because of there trying circumstances I am sure that Ruth and Naomi cried their hearts out at times. But they refused to yield to adversity. And they did not become bitter. They became better. How? Because they trusted and believed that God would make things right in the end.

These simple but heroic women remind us that no matter what we may be going through, no matter how dark the bad news (the unforgiving minute), that we must not lose hope.

You may also want to recall these inspiring lines from John Newton's famous hymn "Amazing Grace" when tragedy, pain, or sorrow come your way:

> 'Twas grace that taught my heart to fear,
> And grace my fears relieved.

How precious did that grace appear
The hour I first believed.

Thro' many dangers, toils, and snares
I have already come.
'Tis grace hath bro't me safe thus far,
And grace will lead me home. (1779)

In sum, when you feel depressed or sad and you need a little extra inspiration or encouragement, remember Ruth's example of courage and resiliency. And then ask yourself what you can learn from this remarkable woman about coping, regenerating, and if necessary reinventing yourself when the bad news – **THE UNFORGIVING MINUTE** –comes your way.

**"If you can fill the unforgiving minute
With sixty seconds' worth of distance run,"**

As a side thought, I want to remind you that if your circumstances or recovery does not turn out the way you want them to, God is still God. And you must trust that He knows what is best for you. Remember, His plan for you may be different than your plan for you. But never doubt that if you keep your hope and faith you will win no matter what obstacles come your way.

I also want to remind you that God promises believers that in their final home there will be no more tears, sorrows, pains, handicaps, or heartaches. For those who are suffering or who have a broken heart, what a great promise to hold on to. (1 Corinthians 15:50-53) (Rev 7:17)

"If you can fill the unforgiving minute
With sixty seconds' worth of distance run,"

§§§

Meditate on These Related Wisdom-Filled Scriptures

"No matter how many times you trip them up, God-loyal people don't stay down long."
Proverbs 24:16 (MSG)

"Many are the afflictions of the righteous; but the Lord delivers him out of them all."
Psalms 34:19 (KJV)

"Do not fear, for I am with you;
Do not anxiously look about you, for I am your God.
I will strengthen you, surely I will help you,
Surely I will uphold you with My righteous right hand."
Isaiah 41:10 (NASB)

"No, in all these things we are more than conquerors through him who loved us."
Romans 8:37 (NIV)

How can you apply these Scriptures to your life?

CHAPTER 15: IF YOU CAN FILL THE UNFORGIVING MINUTE...

Remember, With God's Help:

§§§

- I will not let the bad news (unforgiving minute) devastate me.
- I can deal with the unpredictable.
- I will not be defeated.

Remember to pray …
Dear God, thank you for helping me see the good on the other side of the bad things that happen to me in life as you did for Ruth and Naomi. And help me develop coping skills when I receive that jolt, that shock, the bad news (The unforgiving minute.)

**"If you can fill the unforgiving minute
With sixty seconds' worth of distance run,"**

What did you learn from this chapter?

Chapter 16
Yours is the Earth and everything that's in it, "And – which is more – you'll be a Man, my son!"

The Bible reminds us again, as does Kipling's "If", that we are ultimately the sum of our thoughts, choices, and actions. And, because we are the sum of our thoughts, choices, and actions, we need to remember that there will be a consequence for every choice or decision we make.

> "... for whatever a man sows, this he will also reap."
> (Galatians 6:7, NASB)

Thus, it is imperative that we try to make the right choices and dwell on the right thoughts.

And, one way to help us do this is for us to stay mentally and spiritually focused on the words of Jesus and integrate them into our lives. Jesus reminds us of this with this admonition,

> *"These words I speak to you ...* **If you work the words into your life***, you are like a smart carpenter who dug deep and laid the foundation of his house on bedrock. When the river burst its banks and crashed against the house, nothing could shake it; it was built to last. But if you just use my words in Bible studies and don't work them into your life, you are like the dumb carpenter who built a house but skipped the foundation. When the swollen*

> If you only read the words of "If" and don't work them into your life, what good does it do you?

river came crashing in, it collapsed like a house of cards. It was a total loss" (Luke 6:47-49 MSG, emphasis mine).

James, who was Jesus's brother, echoed Jesus's sentiments when he said, "Do not merely listen to the word ... Do what it says" (James 1:22 NIV).

Paul, the great apostle, also reminds us of the importance of working the Word into our life and thinking the right thoughts. Remember, It is hard to live rightly if you are thinking wrongly.

> Remember that whatever we do or say starts with a thought, which invariably leads to action, reaction, or no action.

Your thoughts can shape your life.

Paul also understood that it is not always easy to control our thoughts. And he reminds us when we do have negative thoughts, we need to ask God to replace them and transform them into thoughts that would be pleasing to Him.

> Solomon noted in Proverbs 23:7, "For as a man thinketh in his heart, so is he." (KJV)

Remember, God is in the transformation business. Paul reminds us of this in Romans 12:2 when he wrote, "Do not conform any longer to the pattern of this world, but be transformed by the renewing of your mind." (NIV) (Do you need to renew your mind?)

Paul even gave us examples of what types of thoughts we should dwell upon. (What thoughts do you dwell upon?) He stated in Philippians 4:8:

> "Finally, brethren, whatsoever things are true,
> whatsoever things are honest,
> whatsoever things are just,
> whatsoever things are pure,
> whatsoever things are lovely,
> whatsoever things are of good report;
> if there be any virtue,
> and if there be any praise,
> think on these things." (KJV)

Many years later, the insightful preacher and writer Norman Vincent Peale noted the importance of thoughts when he wrote, "Change your thoughts, and change your world."

As some anonymous person said in these often-quoted words:

> Remember:
> Your thoughts and moods will determine what kind of day you and those around you will have.

> Watch your thoughts; they become words.
> Watch your words; they become actions.
> Watch your actions; they become habits.
> Watch your habits; they become **Character**.
> Watch your character; it becomes your destiny.

I believe these insightful and challenging thoughts are

CHAPTER 16: YOURS IS THE EARTH...

in harmony with the wisdom found in the Bible and in Kipling's poem "If."

§§§

Remember, when you are dealing with difficult people, facing difficult situations, or contemplating difficult choices, pray for discernment. And look for those inspired and wise individuals who have dealt with similar challenges, and ask what you can learn from them.

> Are you in harmony and at peace with yourself? Can you sleep at night?

To reiterate what the wise author of Proverbs said in Proverbs 13:20, "He who walks with the wise grows wise ..." (NIV)

§§§

As I stated in the introduction, nothing can take the place of the Word and sincere prayer when we are seeking God's will for our lives. And I readily acknowledge that manifesting the behaviors and characteristics found in "If" will not make you a Christian. But if you are a Christian, chances are you will manifest many of the behaviors and virtues found in this character-building and life-enhancing poem. (I hope you agree.)

With these thoughts in mind, have you ever asked yourself what behaviors and personal characteristics a Christian should have? As you might expect, God gives us the answer. (Interestingly, the personal characteristics that God wants us to possess are the by-product of trying to live the life God would want us to live.) He chose His inspired messenger, Paul, to relay them to us.

Paul wrote that believers should manifest and demonstrate:

love,
joy,
peace,
patience,
kindness,
goodness,
faithfulness,
gentleness,
and self-control.
Galatians 5:22-23 (NIV)

Of course, the key question is, do you possess these personal characteristics? And if you do not possess them, you need to ask God to help you acquire them. (I am still struggling with acquiring a few of them myself.)

Just for the sake of instruction, let me emphasize the above attributes in the negative. **For example, a person who has not acquired spiritual maturity will often show:**

no love,
no joy,
no peace,
no patience,
no kindness,
no goodness,
no faithfulness,
no gentleness,
and no self-control.

Now be honest and ask yourself, would you really want to be married or associate on a daily basis with individuals who manifest these negative characteristics? I doubt it.

For teaching and learning purposes, you could also paraphrase the virtues or behaviors that Kipling describes in "If" in the negative. For example, he or she:

> Never keeps their head when a crisis comes
> Never trusts themselves
> Never turns their dreams or thoughts into reality
> Never learns to keep life in perspective
> Never learns to cope with adversities
> Never thinks of others.

I think you get the idea.

A Simple Faith Test

When assessing your faith, look into the mirror, study your face, and remember what the writer of Proverbs wrote, "A happy heart makes the face cheerful." (Proverbs 15:13, NIV) Do you have a cheerful face? If not, why not? Do those around you have a cheerful face, if not, why not?

§§§

As I have alluded to throughout this book, I pray and hope that you will move toward acquiring the life-enhancing and character-building behaviors and virtues described in Kipling's "If" and in Galatians 5:22-23. Of course, in the final analysis, this all depends upon YOU and how much you desire to become the kind of person God wants you to become.

•••••••••••••

Now, as we come to the end of our journey together, I want to thank you, dear friend, for taking time to read this book and for reflecting on my thoughts.

In Closing

May God bless you,
transform you,
direct you,
inspire you,
encourage you,
and give you hope, joy, peace, and tranquility
as you navigate through life.

Notes

About the Author
§§§

Dr. J. Rodney Short is professor emeritus at Texas Woman's University. He received his doctorate in Educational Leadership and Organizational Behavior from the University of Alabama, where he was awarded a graduate fellowship. He was also a men's dormitory Director for the university. Dr. Short believes the key to effective leadership and a productive life is the ability to make wise choices and decisions.

His earlier experiences included a stint as a U.S. Marine, an oilfield roustabout, farmer, lifeguard, coach, teacher and public school and university administrator.

Over the years, Dr. Short has spoken to thousands of people as a motivational/inspirational speaker and has won much recognition for his entertaining, provocative and uplifting speeches. He was the recipient of the Distinguished Mentor Award from the University of Texas Cooperative Superintendency Program.

Because of a dysfunctional family, which resulted in both of his parents being institutionalized at a state psychiatric hospital, and because of the fact that his alcoholic father was found dead in an alley, Dr. Short's passion and interest have revolved around those who have overcome adversities.

You can contact Dr. Short at:
jrskipling@yahoo.com and
www.jrskbooks.com

Cut out, memorize, and post

IF

If you can keep your head when all about you
  Are losing theirs and blaming it on you;
If you can trust yourself when all men doubt you,
  But make allowance for their doubting too:
If you can wait and not be tired by waiting,
  Or, being lied about, don't deal in lies,
Or, being hated, don't give way to hating,
  And yet don't look too good, nor talk too wise;

If you can dream – and not make dreams your master;
  If you can think – and not make thoughts your aim,
If you can meet with Triumph and Disaster
  And treat those two impostors just the same:
If you can bear to hear the truth you've spoken
  Twisted by knaves to make a trap for fools,
Or watch the things you gave your life to, broken,
  And stoop and build'em up with worn-out tools;

If you can make one heap of all your winnings
  And risk it on one turn of pitch-and-toss,
And lose, and start again at your beginnings,
  And never breathe a word about your loss:
If you can force your heart and nerve and sinew
  To serve your turn long after they are gone,
And so hold on when there is nothing in you
  Except the Will which says to them: "Hold on!"

If you can talk with crowds and keep your virtue,
  Or walk with Kings – nor lose the common touch,
If neither foes nor loving friends can hurt you,
  If all men count with you, but none too much:
If you can fill the unforgiving minute
  With sixty seconds' worth of distance run,
Yours is the Earth and everything that's in it,
  And – which is more – you'll be a Man, my son!
– Rudyard Kipling (1910)

                    Compliments of Dr. J. Rodney Short

www.ingramcontent.com/pod-product-compliance
Lightning Source LLC
Chambersburg PA
CBHW061446040426
42450CB00007B/1244